H O L Y   W E E K

**INTERPRETING
THE LESSONS OF
THE CHURCH YEAR**

ROBERT H. SMITH

**PROCLAMATION 5
SERIES A**

FORTRESS PRESS   MINNEAPOLIS

PROCLAMATION 5
Interpreting the Lessons of the Church Year
Series A, Holy Week

Cover and interior design: Spangler Design Team

Library of Congress Cataloging-in-Publication Data

Proclamation 5 : interpreting the lessons of the church year.
    p. cm.
    Contents: ser. A. [1] Epiphany / Pheme Perkins. [2] Holy week /
Robert H. Smith. [3] Advent/Christmas / Mark Allan Powell.
[4] Lent / Cain Hope Felder.
    ISBN 0-8006-4178-7 (ser. A, Epiphany) — ISBN
0-8006-4180-9 (ser. A, Holy week) — ISBN 0-8006-4177-9
(ser. A, Advent/Christmas) — ISBN 0-8006-4179-5 (ser. A, Lent)
    1. Bible—Homiletical use. 2. Bible—Liturgical lessons, English.
BS534.5.P765   1992
251—dc20   92-22973
                                                                    CIP

The paper used in this publication meets the minimum requirements of American National Standard for Information Services—Permanence of Paper for Printed Library Materials, ANSI Z329.48-1984.   ∞™

Manufactured in the U.S.A.   AF 1-4180

96   95   94   93   92   1   2   3   4   5   6   7   8   9   10

CONTENTS

Holy Week Proclamation

The texts of Holy Week are in most cases traditional readings that since the fourth century have been passed down to us as part of the church's spiritual exercises. The following commentaries for each day in Holy Week begin with brief notes about the use of these texts in Jerusalem in the year 384, as reported by a woman named Egeria. She was a pilgrim, and the celebrations in Jerusalem as she describes them involved considerable movement from place to hallowed place.

Taking cues from her identity as a pilgrim and from that early use of the texts in mobile liturgies and moving feasts, I have read all the texts appointed for Holy Week as descriptions of past journeys and as rubrics for our own continuing pilgrimage. I trust that the texts have not suffered too badly, as I have exploited them for language of travel and movement, path and road, even feet and sandals.

Egeria's pilgrimage was an immense undertaking. She left her home in Gaul at the Atlantic coast and traveled east some three thousand miles via Constantinople to spend three years (A.D. 381–384) in Jerusalem and surrounding areas. She kept a record for her "sisters" back home. She and they were members of the same monastic community or, if they were laywomen, of the same pious social circle. Her record, only partially preserved, offers few details of her life. Did she have travel companions? Did she walk or ride? How was it possible for a woman to move about so freely unless she was well connected politically?

Whatever her social class or the circumstances of her journey, Egeria never complains of the rigors of the way. Nor does her account breathe a word concerning what we would call the secular sights along the way: legendary landmarks like storied mountains and rivers or Roman and Greek cities with their public buildings and works of art. Egeria's Bible was her map. She was endlessly curious about the places where events of sacred story happened. She describes those sites for her sisters and speaks glowingly of hospitality received and liturgies celebrated in each place.

Egeria's account of Holy Week worship in Jerusalem is especially rich in detail. Holy Week was known in Egeria's Gallic homeland as the Paschal Week, but she writes that in Jerusalem it was called Great Week, as it still is today among the Orthodox.

Egeria worshiped in Jerusalem at an extraordinary time. Jerome would settle in Bethlehem (six miles away) in the year after her return home, while Cyril was nearing the end of his long tenure as bishop. Cyril had delivered his *Catechetical Lectures* for the first time as a presbyter in 348 and served as bishop of Jerusalem from 350–387.

Cyril was probably born in Jerusalem (ca. 315) and was not yet a teenager when Constantine ordered the construction of a great church complex over the site of Golgotha and Jesus' empty tomb (326). Eusebius of Caesarea preached at the service dedicating the church on September 14, 335.

By the time Egeria arrived in Jerusalem, Holy Week services involved worshipers in movement around the city and up to the Mount of Olives, but services always climaxed inside the city at Constantine's church.

Egeria names three major features of the church complex. The Anastasis is the rotunda built over the tomb at the westernmost end of the complex. Immediately east of the Anastasis was a large open courtyard. In the southwest corner of that colonnaded court stood Golgotha, surmounted by a cross. The eastern end of the courtyard abutted the Constantinian basilica called the Martyrium. (A Crusader building called the Church of the Holy Sepulchre has covered the site since the middle of the twelfth century.)

As bishop of Jerusalem, Cyril took responsibility for physical places in the city's environs hallowed by their connection with events in Jesus' final days. Cyril incorporated those places into the church's calendar and liturgies, weaving an impressive and influential tapestry. Pilgrims were arriving in the Holy Land in increasing numbers, and Cyril's arrangement enabled them to experience sacred sites in an orderly and edifying manner. He also kept the pilgrims under some kind of control.

Pilgrims easily get out of control. Historian Victor Turner and others describe pilgrimage as a deliberate breaking away from routine and mundane structure. A movement away from the ordinary toward the center of holiness, pilgrimage involves a critique of cultural values and the prevailing order. As they lay aside routines and everyday responsibilities, pilgrims cut themselves off from the comforts and protections of their old lives and adopt fresh disciplines. Early Christian pilgrims frequently adopted simplicity of dress and behavior, walking the Roman roads to Palestine even when they had money to ride, abstaining from washing, fasting for days on end. They deliberately set themselves apart from ordinary travelers.

Little wonder that journeys, both real and fictional, loom so large in the annals of humankind: migration, exodus, forced march, voyage of discovery, missionary journey, homecoming. A glance at one card catalog turned up these phrases, both literal and metaphorical, connected with pilgrimages: pilgrimage to Jerusalem, to Rome, to Luther's Germany, to Canterbury; pilgrimage to freedom, to humanity, to truth, to inner space, to now/here; pilgrimage as search, quest, odyssey, and as the opposite of security and possession.

Psychiatrist M. Scott Peck characterizes healthy human life as following the road less traveled. All human beings, he says, are called by God to walk the narrow path to mental and spiritual maturity. Vast numbers of people, however, fail to heed the call, or they respond only feebly, because the way to reality is not easy, and they lack the necessary discipline to undertake the journey.

In the New Testament, each Gospel opens with a report of pilgrimage. Matthew tells how Magi journeyed from a distant land to lay their gifts before the child of Bethlehem. Mark describes how the people of Jerusalem and Judea, drawn by the prophetic power of John, left their homes and gathered at the Jordan to receive baptism in preparation for the coming sovereignty of God. Luke pictures Mary (alone and on foot?) traveling to the hill country of Judea to meet Elizabeth, where, at the end of that journey, the unborn John greeted the unborn Jesus.

In the Gospel of John, the first words out of the mouth of Jesus are spoken to two disciples of the Baptist who had begun to follow him. He asked, "What are you seeking?" The question is really addressed to each reader: "By all your reading and all your living, what are you looking for? What is the goal of your life?"

The life of Jesus in the Synoptic Gospels is a single swift campaign of preaching and healing, sweeping through Galilee and climaxing at the temple in Jerusalem. Jesus traveled the narrow way and summoned people to follow his path. In John's Gospel Jesus says simply, "I am the real and living way" (14:6).

Early believers, before the word *Christian* was invented, were known as "people belonging to the Way" (Acts 9:2). Pilgrimage, then, is a particular form of intentional travel. It is time out for the time being, time to reflect on the totality of our journeying through time and space. The pilgrimage toward wholeness and holiness serves as the organizing theme for this book on the readings of Holy Week.

"wholeness" = holiness?

Sunday of the Passion
Palm Sunday

Lutheran	Roman Catholic	Episcopal	Common Lectionary
Isa. 50:4-9a	Isa. 50:4-7	Isa. 45:21-25	Isa. 50:4-9a
Phil. 2:5-11	Phil. 2:6-11	Phil. 2:5-11	Phil. 2:5-11
Matt. 26:1—27:66	Matt. 26:14—27:66	Matt. 27:1-54	Matt. 26:14—27:66 or Matt. 27:11-54

Which is it? Palm Sunday or Passion Sunday? Can we have it both ways? In some places the palm procession is hors d'oeuvres, lightweight food to nibble on before the main dish is served. Viewed as an amusing preliminary, it delights children and their adoring parents. Afterward we all hunker down in our pews and put our minds to the more solemn business of the Eucharist, introduced by the reading of the entire passion according to Matthew. A joyous procession followed by an abrupt shift to a minor key can be defended. The mood shifted just that way in Jesus' last days in Jerusalem. Perhaps the change reflects also the chronic fickleness of the church: greeting him with palms and loud hosannas one moment and crying "crucify him!" the next.

Yet viewing the Palms and Passion as a single event yields a single complex truth: victory through suffering. This Sunday trumpets the fact that Christ's enthronement occurs through his passion and not without it. The triumphant Christ is the crucified Christ and no other.

Starting near Bethany on the Mount of Olives, Jesus entered Jerusalem from the east, from the place of the rising sun. At nearly the same moment Pontius Pilate was entering the city from the direction of the setting sun, leading his troops up from the provincial capital at Caesarea by the sea.

Crowds greeted Jesus with branches cut from olive trees and palm, a marvelous mix of greenery symbolizing both peace and victory, an elusive combination. Only John's Gospel pictures the crowds of Jerusalem as thronging to see Jesus, because they had heard what he had done for Lazarus, and they were eager to stand in the presence of this life-giver. Pilate arrived with officers and troops of Caesar's legions bearing their instruments of death. Pilate's company covered the eagles on their standards out of deference to Jewish sensibilities regarding such carved images, but they made no effort to sheath their swords or hide their spears of iron.

Named together in the Apostles' Creed, these two leaders, Jesus and Pontius Pilate, with their contrasting entourages, represent vastly different ways of organizing all of life. Both bid us to follow in their train. The last days of Jesus show how futile it is to think of walking both paths at once. The way that Jesus travels was shunned by his friends (Judas and Peter) and viciously attacked by his foes (the elders of the people and Pilate). Yet Jesus' path is the road to life and glory, not only at the end, but each step of the way.

Egeria records that in Jerusalem at the beginning of Great Week worshipers gather on the slopes of the Mount of Olives at the Eleona Church (*Eleona* means "of the Mount of Olives") early in the afternoon. At three o'clock all climb to the summit to the Imbomon, a hillock marking the spot from which Jesus had ascended into heaven. There they sing psalms and pray in the open air. A few years later, in 392, another woman, Poimenia, a wealthy pilgrim, erected a church there.

At five in the afternoon, carrying branches of palm or olive, they descend the mount while chanting Psalm 118 with v. 26 as antiphon, "Blessed is he who comes in the name of the Lord." Parents with children on their shoulders, commoners and people of rank, clergy and lay people form one festal troop. They move with the bishop down the mount, across the Kidron Valley, up into the city, and through its winding streets until they stand together in the Martyrium, Constantine's basilica.

In his *Catechetical Lectures* (10:19), Cyril claims that it was still possible to see the very palm trees that supplied the branches waved by children at Jesus' first entrance. That tree was also noted by the Pilgrim of Bordeaux (333), thus indicating that it was a popular feature of Jerusalem piety in the early fourth century.

Palms have captured the Christian imagination, in spite of the fact that palm branches are mentioned only in John's Gospel (12:13) and not in the Synoptics, which speak more vaguely of "leafy branches cut in the fields" (Mark 11:8). Is it possible at this late date to recover the use of olive branches on "Palm Sunday"? They would help to define the character of our pilgrimage and the nature of the triumph we seek: the Lord's peace. Olive branches are an ancient tradition, and their reintroduction and use alongside the palms of victory would be well worth the effort.

What kind of parade on Palm Sunday would capture the rich reality of God's own life in our time and space? It would have to be deliberately and assertively diverse. Would it include baby carriages and wheelchairs and the shopping carts of the poor? Should worshipers walk with birds in cages and dogs on leashes, carrying potted plants in their hands? How else can we signal that earth supports our pilgrimage and that we walk in the company of plants and animals as fellow creatures? The procession should not be mere playacting, miming the entrance of Jesus to Jerusalem. It should speak somehow of our own odyssey.

Searching for the holy, pilgrims discover a new community transcending old limits of tongue and nation. In Egeria's Holy Week services, the bishop, flanked by presbyters, speaks Greek (the language of Bible and liturgy) while the priests offer almost simultaneous translation into Syriac, the native tongue of most Christians in the holy land, and into Latin for the sake of pilgrims like herself. When Jerome (just a few years later) writes of the nationalities of pilgrims in the Holy Land (Letter 46), his list reads like the roll call of nations in Peter's Pentecost sermon.

In 1991 Christians were found marching in demonstrations for and against war in the Persian Gulf, for and against abortion. They clearly signal their positions. Our Palm Sunday procession should be equally clear in declaring who we are, with whom we travel, whom we follow, and what our goal is.

GOSPEL: MATTHEW 26–27

The Judge Is Judged (26:1-2)

Matthew's passion narrative begins here, but it really helps to move back and start with the immediately preceding paragraph (25:31-46). In that final paragraph of his fifth and final discourse in Matthew's Gospel, Jesus pictures himself as great shepherd and judge at the end of history. All the nations will stand before his throne, and he will divide them into sheep at his right hand and goats at his left. In reporting that vision (it is not a parable), Jesus declares in unforgettable fashion the criteria he will apply in judging.

In the passion narrative Jesus stands powerless, a helpless prisoner under the judgment of a human court, working with far different

standards of guilt and innocence. The judge is judged and badly so—
a jarring juxtaposition of images.

As Jesus marches toward the cross, Matthew pictures him as living
and dying in accord with the standards he has announced in his vision:
He gives bread and quenches thirst with wine (26:26-29), confers
benefits on homeless strangers (27:7) and on a notorious prisoner (27:15-
23), and yields up his garments to clothe others while he himself goes
naked (27:35).

Friends and Enemies (26:3-75)

26:3-16. Verses 3-5 and 14-16 are a beginning and an end, embracing
6-13, the center of a deliciously ironic sandwich. Men of the temple
and of his own circle (3-5, 14-16) are eager to hasten Jesus on his path
to death and, they presume, his everlasting extinction. But a nameless
woman (6-13) in the calm eye of that storm anoints his body. She
honors him with her gift and enters into his dying with her own most
extravagant outpouring. (Further comments at 26:20-35; cf. John 12:1-
11, Monday.)

26:17-19. Jesus' prophetic foresight concerning the place of his last
supper is another reminder (like 26:1-2) of his mastery, even though
he seems to be poor clay in the grip of other people and their manip-
ulations.

26:20-35. Paragraphs about Judas "the Great Traitor" (20-25) and
about Peter "the Great Denier" (30-35) surround the central passage
about Jesus "the Great Giver" (26-29). (Matthew 26:3-35 is further
treated on Wednesday.)

The words and actions of Jesus at table (26:26-29) parallel the
gestures of the nameless woman at that other table (26:3-13). The
woman, like Jesus, is a champion giver. She shares Jesus' vision of
God's sovereignty as a government of giving. Her actions mirror ahead
of time his own breaking of bread (and body) and pouring out of wine
(and blood). Without a word, she offers her dramatic gesture, snapping
the alabaster flask and pouring out its ointment. Later, with words
forever graven on the church's memory, Jesus will tear the loaf in pieces
and spill out the wine, offering them up to be consumed. His handful
of words interpret that bread and wine and all his living as grace and
nourishment for others.

Matthew earlier related another memorable table scene that stands
in stark contrast to the episodes of the nameless woman and of Jesus'

last supper. Herod at his own birthday party (14:1-12), surrounded by his cronies and clients, uttered rash words and had to offer up the head of John the Baptist on a serving dish.

Unlike Herod, the nameless woman and Jesus are givers, not takers, of life. Sharing life is healthful and healing. It alone makes people all right. In scene after scene Matthew presses readers to receive that power and walk in it.

26:36-56. Two episodes (36-56 and 57-75) confirm the predictions made by Jesus concerning Peter and Judas. Neither of these disciples understands why Jesus walks a path leading to the cross. These two are not alone: "All the disciples forsook him and fled" (26:56). They rush off, seeking safer pathways.

Jesus dedicates himself to the Father's will and the drinking of the cup (36-46). When one disciple betrays and another swings his weapon, Jesus comments memorably on swords and power (47-56). He will not ask the Father for twelve legions. He will not play Rome's game. As in the temptations in the wilderness, Jesus renounces the way of wealth and power. He is no Herod the Great, slaughterer of children (2:16-18), no Herod Antipas, killer of the Baptist (14:1-12). He will not live at the expense of others. His path is trust and love.

Wealth without love and power without justice—these are demonic. Jesus renounces acquisitiveness and turns his back on control over others. His is the vulnerable authority of love.

26:57-75. The priests' plot (26:1-2, 14-16) and the narration of the disciples' failure (26:20-25, 30-35, 36-46, 47-56) connect at 26:57-58. This pericope (57-75) is generally understood as reciting the contrast between Peter and Jesus. But actually it declares the combined, terrible assault of insiders and outsiders on "the Christ, the Son of God" (v. 63). Friends and foes alike are moved by the same thirst for power and position. They fear losing their own individual or national lives, and so they join in rejecting the strange sovereignty of grace. Both disciples and enemies recoil from him. Friends and foes alike wash their hands and banish him from their lives.

Judgments on Jesus (27:1-31)

27:1-10. Just when it seems that Jesus is most alone and powerless, flashes of lightning pierce the dark. The announcement of the collusion of native and foreign powers in 27:1-2, 11-14 brackets the astonishing

11

note regarding Judas (3-10). At the most unlikely moment Judas "repented." This is the real thing (cf. 21:29). He comes to his senses and testifies to Jesus' innocence.

In meditating on Judas' fate and the money he handed back, Matthew ponders the power of Jesus' blood. This is one in a series of passages on blood, beginning back in 26:28 ("blood of the covenant"). Here "blood money" returned by Judas purchases a "field of blood," where poor strangers find a final resting place. The blood of Jesus benefits strangers, the powerless, and the marginal. Jesus, in his dying as in his living, conforms to the contours of his own final teaching (cf. 25:31-46).

27:15-23. The choice between power as defined by Barabbas and as exhibited by Jesus is familiar from Mark. Matthew sharpens the ironies by writing that people were summoned to decide which of these two is the real Jesus. Is it Jesus-Barabbas or Jesus-Messiah? Which of them is the bringer of salvation? (see Matt. 1:21). Which one is pioneer and pathfinder for us?

Unique to Matthew is the note concerning Pilate's wife. At the precise moment when the governor was to render a verdict from his official rostrum, he received word that she had had a dream (channel of divine revelation, cf. Matthew 1–2) about Jesus. She counseled: "Do not move against that righteous man" (25:37, 46; 3:15; 5:20). She is the second woman in this narrative with an insight into Jesus not given to the men (cf. 26:6-13).

27:24-26. Pilate washed his hands, and "all the people" cried out, " 'His blood be on us and upon our children.' " Repeatedly in history this cry has provoked anti-Jewish outbursts. It should instead evoke the haunting memory of Jesus' own words concerning the profound benefits of his blood on the heads of all human beings (26:28; cf. 27:3-10). Part of our pilgrimage in Holy Week must be to see if we can find ways of dissociating ourselves from unhealthy ways of reading Scripture (anti-Jewish, antihomosexual, antiforeigner). This week is opportunity to renew our commitment to the way of Christ, who pours out his life's blood "for all."

27:27-31. The language of kingship, hurled as an accusation against Jesus in 11-14, is taken up again as soldiers submit Jesus to a mock enthronement. How can this poor figure be "the king of the Jews" (and of everyone else)? How can he be the sovereign leader to life?

His is a sovereignty based on the gracious outpouring of his own blood in a flood of forgiveness (cf. 26:28). His government stands in awful contrast to sovereignty founded on the sword of the legionnaire (26:53; cf. 2:16-18; 14:1-12) or on the venality and criminality of a Barabbas (27:15-26). While nature and culture seem to scream the message that it is necessary to hate the enemy, Jesus dies rather than hate or kill (5:43-48).

Crucified, Dead, and Buried (27:32-60)

27:32-50. In all three of Matthew's crucifixion scenes, God is named: Invoked by crucifiers (27:32-34), addressed in prayer by Jesus (45-50), confessed by the centurion and his squad (51-54). To the crucifiers God means power, and Jesus in no way resembles a "son" of God. In the central scene Jesus struggles with his own vocation and relationship with God. In the third scene God disturbs the theology of the crucifiers and responds to Jesus' cry, as the earth shakes and splits, and the centurion is shocked into his awed exclamation.

27:51-60. At the moment of Jesus' death, a gentile centurion confesses him, and saints of the first testament rise from their tombs (51-54). Jesus' death begins to ransom many from the grip of deadly tyrants (20:28; 27:9-10).

At the same moment readers learn of the presence of women who had "followed" Jesus from Galilee, serving him; their names are recited (55-56). From where did Joseph of Arimathea, "a disciple of Jesus," come (57-60)?

For the moment, the twelve insiders forsake Jesus, but God draws others to him, raising them up from nothing, even from slumbers in their tombs. God can raise up children to Abraham from stones of the wilderness (Matt. 3:9), and from equally unlikely sources God raises up women and men to follow Jesus on his path.

FIRST LESSON: ISAIAH 50:4-9
GOD'S SERVANT

Since the work of Bernhard Duhm at the beginning of this century (1902), four poems in Isaiah have been identified as "Suffering Servant Songs": Isa. 42:1-7; 49:1-7; 50:4-9; 52:13—53:12. All four are appointed for reading during Holy Week.

The songs were composed while Israel was exiled in Babylon. They first circulated around 545 B.C.E., when the Babylonian empire was showing signs of fatigue. That weakening of Babylon signaled the dawning of new possibilities for exiles.

Who is the servant? The nation of Israel in its mission among the nations? A remnant within Israel, faithful to the ancient covenant? A suffering prophet like Jeremiah? The prophet Isaiah with his circle of disciples? Scholars dispute the possibilities.

At least two things need to be said about our uncertainties. First, the mystery surrounding the identity of the servant may help us to read the songs as pointing both to Jesus as an individual figure and to the whole people of God, both before and after Jesus. We may distinguish, but it is not healthy to separate, the way of Jesus from the way of God's people. Second, our difficulties regarding the identity of the servant may turn us to more useful questions: What are we to learn from the servant concerning power and suffering and God?

50:4. The servant is summoned to a mission of speech. God has given to the servant "the tongue of those who are taught," and each day attunes the servant's ears to the most profound music of the universe: the whispering of God amid the chatter of the nations and the world's roaring. The world loves its old tunes, its words, its comfortable myths. But God commissions the servant to "sustain the weary" (cf. Isa. 40:29-31; Matt. 11:28-30) by the uncomfortable wisdom of God.

50:5. In tune with God, the servant moved unswervingly along the appointed path. His feet did not rebel, and he "did not turn backward." This note of stubborn fidelity is echoed later in Philippians, where it is said that Jesus was obedient all the way to death, "even death on a cross."

50:6. In tune with God, out of sync with the world, he encountered troubling resistance. The graphic description of enmity and insult is the reason this poem is read also on Wednesday of this week, when betrayal by Judas is the traditional theme.

50:7-8a. On Palm/Passion Sunday it is most fitting to meditate on the defiance and resolve exhibited in the words "I have set my face like flint" (Luke 9:51). Surrounded by scoffers, the servant always presses forward on his way, never looking back.

50:8. What is the secret of his strength? The sure knowledge that God will vindicate him. Enemies surround him like so many false witnesses, spouting their accusations. But the servant brims with the confidence that Yahweh is his jury, advocate, and judge (see Rom. 8:31-39).

50:9. The servant stands in Yahweh's court and cares nothing for any human verdict. All his now-powerful enemies will in time fall apart like rotten cloth.

ALTERNATIVE FIRST LESSON: ISAIAH 45:21-25

Babylon, the very model of arrogant politics, collapsed almost overnight. God challenges the survivors to state once more their old proud boasts about the power of their gods. Who foresaw their downfall? Idols of wood and iron? No! Only Yahweh! "There is no other god besides me!"

God does not gloat over Babylon's defeat. God would be a righteous God, and that means Savior for all. God speaks tender invitation: "Turn to me and be saved, all the ends of the earth!"

God who created all has sworn an oath for the good of all: "To me every knee shall bow and every tongue shall swear" (Phil. 2:10-11; Rom. 14:11).

SECOND LESSON: PHILIPPIANS 2:5-11
HE EMPTIED HIMSELF

Here Paul quotes one of a number of hymns that circulated alongside the Psalms in the gatherings of the earliest Christian communities. It is a superb choice for today, partly because it describes Jesus' career as a great cosmic journey, and partly because it climaxes in a doxology like those that worshipers around the world shout aloud to the Christ on Palm Sunday.

In fact, the text assumes that Palm Sunday worshipers in Connecticut and California do not only join other Christian people gathered everywhere around the globe, waving palms and singing, "All Glory, Laud, and Honor." More than that, they are caught up into the worship rendered by all creatures in the heavens and on earth and under the earth. All together bend the knee and acclaim him Lord. The care of the Lord extends to every creature, and the climax of the way of the Lord is thus not just a new humanity but a new creation. All creatures will sing the new tune in perfect harmony with one another.

The hymn has two stanzas. In 2:5-8 Jesus is the subject, moving relentlessly downward; in 2:9-11 God is the subject, lifting Jesus upward beyond all heights. What is the meaning of this awesome parabola of salvation? What word does the downward-upward path of Jesus speak to us about Jesus and about God? We here confront the fundamental mystery at the heart of all New Testament meditation and proclamation: the paradox that Jesus of Nazareth, a powerless failure, now sits at the right hand of God.

Verses 5-8 contemplate the downward path. It was nothing forced on Jesus by circumstances of birth, want of ability, poverty of the times, lack of opportunity, or the oppressive character of the system. His way was freely chosen.

At the start he was "in the form of God." That is usually taken as a description of Jesus' preexistence: Before the incarnation he dwelt in light unapproachable as one with God. Alternatively "in the form of God" may mean that he was a human being, made like all others "in the image of God." According to the former picture, he did not selfishly cling to what he had as the preexistent one. In the latter picture, he did not try to seize by violence what was not his. In either case, he did not exploit for selfish ends his status with God (as preexistent being or as human made in God's image).

Instead of "puffing himself up" in arrogant fashion (1 Cor. 4:6, 18-19; 5:2; 8:1) he "emptied himself." Jesus did not spend his days attempting to carve out for himself the largest possible comfort zone; rather he "humbled himself." He lived his life in fullest obedience to God, and that means in closest communion with the creative mystery at the heart of all of life. He sustained that obedience all the days of his brief journey, and that was far from easy, because his path led relentlessly to the hard wood of the cross.

This first stanza of the hymn is the entire biography of Jesus writ small. This was his whole life: the steady, selfless submission of all his energies and substance to the will of God. Never was there even the merest hint of a gap between the will of Jesus and the will of God. In another hymn Paul defines the will of Jesus and the will of God. Its name is *agape*, or love (1 Corinthians 13).

2:9-11. In the first stanza, Jesus acts toward God; in the second, God acts toward Jesus. In response to the willing obedience of Jesus, God "superexalted" him and graciously bestowed on him a "name" (meaning reality and substance) that outranks every other. That name is Lord.

God summons all creatures great and small, whatever place they hold throughout the length and breadth of the universe, to bend their knees and lift their voices in the confession "Jesus Christ is Lord!" Citizens of the empire hailed their Caesars and by their blended voices and allegiances constructed the reality of the Roman Empire. Just so, Christians salute Jesus of Nazareth, cross and all. By their shared confession they bring into being a new social reality under his governance.

The church at Philippi, fractured by rivalries, needed to hear again how humility and mutual self-giving actualize the new creation. By exalting Jesus, Lover of creation and Servant of God, God exalts self-giving, God enthrones agape, God glorifies the mutual care of one for the other. That is what Paul read in this hymn, and that is why he uses it here. By means of this hymn Paul hopes to shatter the old world ruled by principalities and powers and to construct a new world governed by agape.

Although the phrase "God the Father" in this hymn is grating for many today, sensitized to androcentric connotations and patriarchal abuses, the hymn concludes in this fashion precisely to rectify common misconceptions. It celebrates the revelation of the lordship of God in Jesus of Nazareth as contrast and antidote to all systems in which God and the gods are defined in terms of domination and oppression.

In Jesus we see not just a Galilean sage or charismatic rabbi or eccentric prophet but none other than God. Most important, we do not see God conforming to the definitions humans ordinarily assign to the word *God*. Words like *power* (even *omnipotence*) and *knowledge* (even *omniscience*) are not found here. Rather, we see God offering a fresh definition of the habits of the divine heart. In Jesus we see God exercising the divine lordship by bending down and loving an oppressed creation into newness of life.

Monday in Holy Week

Lutheran	Roman Catholic	Episcopal	Common Lectionary
Isa. 42:1-9	Isa. 42:1-7	Isa. 42:1-9	Isa. 42:1-9
Heb. 9:11-15		Heb. 11:39—12:3	Heb. 9:11-15
John 12:1-11	John 12:1-11	John 12:1-11 *or* Mark 14:3-9	John 12:1-11

Egeria does not say what Scripture was read on Monday of Holy Week, but early in the next century the day was observed with a late afternoon service featuring Matt. 20:17-28 (Armenian lectionary). The mother of James and John seeks places of honor for her sons, imagining that the way of freedom and life leads upward to the pinnacle of the pyramid of power.

In response, Jesus speaks of his own downward way as a joyous path, freely chosen. Matthew 20:17-28 interprets the path of Jesus through Holy Week as at once both creational and countercultural. It is creational because it is life in harmony with God and with humanity's own true being, and so it is a path of peace, wholeness, and joy. It is counter-cultural because it rubs against the grain and is the opposite of everything that James and John and their doting mother seek. Jesus renews the call to his disciples, bidding them to join him on his way. He invites them to share his path of joy.

Our modern lectionaries offer different Scriptures for this day, but they too are commentaries on the path of Jesus. Isaiah 42 describes the servant's path as outward-bound, bearing justice to the remotest edges of the inhabited world. Hebrews 9 portrays the crucified as upward-bound to the heart of the universe, drawing near to God. John 12 portrays the anointing of Jesus' feet, as he walks toward Jerusalem and the goal of his way.

GOSPEL: JOHN 12:1-11
HOW BEAUTIFUL THE FEET

The path of Jesus is strewn with sharper stuff than garments and branches laid down by adoring crowds. He marches a hard and narrow way (Matt. 7:13-14) toward a fatal confrontation. But he is no accidental tourist. He has elected his path in full awareness of the cost.

Mary of Bethany celebrates the road that Jesus goes, while Judas cannot see it as anything but the way of ruin. In John's narrative, Jesus will walk his path and enter Jerusalem as one oddly anointed. Samuel, that ancient maker and breaker of kings, emptied his horn of oil on David's head. Here a woman smears precious ointment on the feet of Jesus. The young shepherd lad of the house of Jesse was an unlikely choice, and so is the son of Mary and Joseph.

In the first century, perfume vases were small vessels with long, slender necks, proud necks, stiff necks. To use the perfume, the owner snapped the neck of the vase and got on with the business of anointing. By her dramatic gesture, Mary (John 12) rejects the proud quest for prestige that marked the mother of James and John (Matthew 20).

By pouring out her oil, Mary of Bethany is marking Jesus for high kingship and for an early grave. Jesus praises her act as her affirmation of the path he is traveling. Jesus is anointed to walk what the evangelist John calls an ascending road, a path to glory, the way of oneness with God, culminating in his being lifted up on the cross. Mary knows and honors the way he walks, while Judas balks, barking sharp dissent.

The odor of that perfume fills the whole house, as the light of this strange king goes forth to the ends of the earth, breaking chains and breathing life (see Isaiah 42).

Mary's act was no small extravagance. A day laborer could have supported himself and his family for an entire year on three hundred denarii. Mary's deed shines all the more brilliantly in contrast to the cheating heart of Judas and of all whose primary aim is acquisition.

Once again a woman comprehends the heart of Jesus and his enterprise. Judas came to see Jesus as his enemy, but not Mary. To her Jesus does not represent some harsh patriarchal deity. She does not recoil as though he has come to impose another odious rule on her and her sisters.

Over the centuries the name of Jesus has certainly been invoked to control women and to "keep them in their place." Many women have experienced Bible, church, and Jesus as the enemy. But Mary affirmed Jesus. She anointed his feet, for she saw in him one whose feet upon the mountains are beautiful. She greeted him as the messenger of peace, proclaiming good news, telling Zion that old tyrannies are nearing their demise (Isa. 52:7).

She anointed his feet, and he will wash his disciples' feet (13:5) to make them ready to walk with him on his path, an invitation that Judas will refuse by lifting his heel against Jesus (13:18), a gesture of utmost contempt and hostility.

FIRST LESSON: ISAIAH 42:1-9
JOURNEYING TOWARD NEW CREATION

God is on a journey, moving from old things toward new things, from creation fallen to creation made new. God has formed us the way a potter shapes a vase for holding ointment (Isa. 45:9; Gen. 2:7), the way a metalworker hammers an ingot and stretches it out to fashion a wonderfully thin sheet of bronze (Isa. 44:12, 24). Just so, God is laying hands on the world once more, hammering and massaging it into new life.

As the poem opens (42:1), God points the finger, publicly commissioning the servant. The task is heavy, but the Lord will sustain the servant in the midst of hard going. Whatever the signs to the contrary may be, the servant has been selected by God (as Gideon and Moses, Saul and David were chosen), is bound to God with cords of love, and is moved by God's own Spirit (cf. Isa. 11:1). These words and themes are echoed in Jesus' baptism (cf. Mark 1:11), as well as in the Gospel for this day (John 12).

Three times (42:1, 3, 4) the poem declares that the servant's task is to "bring forth" or "establish justice," and that means nothing less than to make the world "all right," as it was in the beginning.

The sphere of the servant's work is not narrowly confined to the soul or psyche or to Israel or the church alone. The mission is worldwide, holding in its embrace all continents and islands (cf. 40:4; 15:5). Precisely because the mission is so comprehensive, the servant will appear too weak. He is no Cyrus, no Alexander, no Caesar. He is soft-spoken. The servant is gentle, not one to snap bruised reeds or quench dimly burning wicks (42:2-3).

Is the servant-messiah equal to the task? We need to ask how the cross of Jesus Christ, repulsive emblem of the final weakness known as death, can be paradoxically so attractive and effective in our own lives, assuming that it is. How does it accomplish its work?

The other side of the same question is whether sheer power is able to establish justice and wholeness. Having experienced the force of

Roman arms, a British chieftain remarked, "The Romans create a desert and call it peace." Israeli journalist Jacobo Timmerman, viewing Tyre and Sidon, reduced to rubble by Israeli bombardment during the war in Lebanon, remarked caustically on the Pax Hebraica. Closer to home, questions have been raised about the Pax Americana in the wake of U.S. destruction of Iraq's infrastructure with the ensuing spread of illness among Iraqi children (which some label biological warfare).

To establish justice is first of all an iconoclastic task. It involves ripping blinders from people's eyes, so that they face up to their idols. God weeps to see people on their knees before idols. Idols may be carved from wood, beaten from metal, fashioned from clay, sewn on cloth as flags, or printed on paper by treasury department presses. They cannot grant peace or wholeness. (It is strange that we by turns worship and abuse the stuff of earth.)

God, who created all things out of nothing in the beginning, who in primeval darkness whispered the words (no need to shout), "Light, come and shine!" has sent the servant with light for the nations, to liberate and to cure the blindness of all peoples (42:6-7; John 8:12; Matt. 5:14).

The Servant Songs and the passion narrative, the history of Israel and the story of the Christian church, show that the pilgrimage toward the light is no easy thing for God or for human beings. God yearns to set people free. God aches to plant their feet firmly on the path of light. God stoops painfully to breathe new life into a creaking creation.

SECOND LESSON: HEBREWS 9:11-15
INNER SANCTUM OF THE UNIVERSE

(Hebrews 11:39—12:3, appointed by the Episcopal lectionary, is treated on Wednesday.)

Hebrews 9:11-15 (like Phil. 2:5-11, Sunday's epistle), describes the way of Jesus as a journey: all the way down and through and then all the way up again. Neither Hebrews nor Philippians is content to sketch Jesus' journey as a short walk down the hill of Olives and then up to the hill of Golgotha.

Hebrews 9 describes the way of Jesus in terms of the annual journey of the high priest. Once a year the high priest would penetrate the temple step by sanctified step through zones of increasing holiness in a process of steady separation from everything unclean, until finally he entered the inner sanctum. There in the Holy of Holies the priest stood before the cherubim brooding over the mercy seat, visible footstool of the invisible God. The priest would reach out and smear precious blood on the golden lid of the ark of the covenant and so reconnect God and people, renewing the bond of peace for one more year.

Hebrews pictures Jesus as the ultimate High Priest of the whole universe. He ascends along a cosmic path, penetrating ever upward through encircling spheres, past every curtain and barrier, all the way into the sanctuary of heaven itself, into the inner sanctum of God's eternal throne room (cf. 10:19-20). The death of Jesus scrubs cleaner than the blood of all the old animal sacrifices. His blood pierces the surface of the body and gets under the skin. It reaches all the way down until it touches the conscience, so that women and men may at last appear before God with "truth in the inward parts" (Psalm 51).

Cleansed from dead works, those who belong to Christ offer lively worship. Theirs is a new liturgy, described in summary fashion at the end of this section of Hebrews: Their feet step along a new and living way; they tread a path toward the sanctuary above (the heart of God) in the confidence of faith; they move ceaselessly forward and upward in hope; they always consider how to provoke fellow wayfarers to deeds of love (10:22-24). Such is the liturgy of pilgrims according to Hebrews.

Tuesday in Holy Week

Lutheran	Roman Catholic	Episcopal	Common Lectionary
Isa. 49:1-6	Isa. 49:1-6	Isa. 49:1-6	Isa. 49:1-7
1 Cor. 1:18-25		1 Cor. 1:18-31	1 Cor. 1:18-31
John 12:20-36	John 13:21-33, 36-38	John 12:37-50 or 42-50 or Mark 11:15-19	John 12:20-36

On Tuesday of Holy Week, writes Egeria, Jerusalem Christians assemble late at night on the Mount of Olives at the Eleona Church (the Church of the Mount of Olives). The Eleona Church was built directly over a cave identified by early tradition as the place where Jesus taught his disciples during the final week of his early sojourn. In Egeria's time the church and cave were associated with Jesus' final discourse, recorded in Matthew 24–25. The bishop enters the cave (immediately below the chancel) and, standing inside it, reads aloud those chapters of Matthew's Gospel to the worshipers. Egeria takes those chapters to be commentary on the opening words, "See that no one leads you astray" (Matt. 24:4), a sobering thought during any Holy Week or in the course of any pilgrimage.

The lessons currently assigned to Tuesday of Holy Week focus on the faithfulness of Jesus, while tomorrow's lessons feature the waywardness of Judas.

Later tradition declared that cave, described by Egeria, to be the place where Jesus taught his disciples the Lord's Prayer, and this later tradition has managed to drive out the earlier. Today the place is marked by the Church of the Pater Noster (Our Father). Its cloistered walls are decorated with ceramic tiles bearing the Lord's Prayer in sixty-two languages.

It would certainly be useful to spend Tuesday of Holy Week meditating on the Lord's Prayer. It is the prayer offered by Jesus for the daily journey of all his followers. It is itself daily bread, words able to nourish hearts that grow weary when the way seems hard or absurd. Although not recorded in Mark or John, the Lord's Prayer echoes through Jesus' prayer in Gethsemane (Mark 14:32-42) and in the parallel here in John 12.

Two prayers of Jesus (John 12:27-28 and John 17) bracket the farewell discourses (John 13-16). Both are prayers of the dedication of self to the journey of holiness.

GOSPEL: JOHN 12:20-36
GLORY, GRAIN, AND THE GATHERING

The Greeks, the Glory, and a Grain of Wheat
(John 12:20-26)

The mounting resistance of "the Jews" and now the approach of "some Greeks" signal the end of an old time and the opening of a new history. "Jews" means God's own beloved people, and "Greeks" means outsiders, unclean and contaminating. When Jesus hears that "Greeks" wish "to see" him, he cries out that the world stands at the crossroads. He reads the friendly approach of inquiring Gentiles as a sign that his long-delayed "hour" has now arrived (2:4; 7:30; 8:20; 13:1; 17:1). He has irrupted in the world precisely for this ingathering, this colossal boundary-crossing.

But it is no easy matter. It is never simple to set aside ancient antagonisms and inherited taboos. The line between Jew and Gentile had been set in place in ages past, not by any human hand but by God's own decree.

How can all the varied sheep become one flock (10:16)? How can all God's scattered children be gathered into one (11:52)?

In John's Gospel, that great mission is accomplished at the cross, and therefore the cross is Jesus' glory. The moment of his dying is the "hour" of his "glorification." At the cross he writes, "Gloriously finished!" to the task set him by God (17:1, 5; 19:30).

The rhetoric of Jesus shifts abruptly, and he begins to speak in words reminiscent of the great parable of the sower (Mark 4; Matthew 13; Luke 8). For Mark, sower and seed teach a lesson on the hidden growth and ultimate success of God's strange sovereignty. For Matthew, the parable is full of ethical encouragement, tracing what happens when good seed meets good soil. For Luke, the same parable promises a church growing irresistibly.

John has his own angle of discernment. The Johannine Jesus uses the image of the seed to speak of the mystery of the cross: Life that yields itself up in love, far from being destroyed, engenders even more life. The Christian path is seen in the journey of a single grain of wheat, fulfilling its purpose as it is thrown from the sower's hand and travels a downward path onto the ground and into the ground. Buried in the earth, the seed loses its old life, gives up its former size and shape with all its substance. It is not destroyed but mysteriously transformed. Suddenly it springs upright as a stalk of wheat, heavy with the fruit of many seeds.

Cyril, bishop of Jerusalem in Egeria's time, spoke of the cross as the tree of life. From the tree of Eden came sin, and until the tree of the cross, sin ruled (*Lectures* 13.19). The cross was planted in the earth so that the ground, once cursed, might enjoy fresh blessing and might release all the dead held in its embrace (13.35). Indeed, on Good Friday Jesus was planted in the ground and sprang up as the true Vine, rooting out the curse that came because of Adam (14.11).

The Glory and the Gathering (John 12:27-36)

John continues his meditation on Jesus' dying, again interpreting it as the moment of his glorification. The evangelist takes his cue from the mode of Jesus' execution. Jesus was not sentenced to die by drowning or strangulation, by beheading or stoning. All of those were possibilities in the ancient Roman and Jewish world. Jesus died on a cross.

To John, the mode of Jesus' dying is no accident. He sees a divine truth articulated in the method of execution. Crucifixion means that the feet of Jesus, which had walked the paths of Galilee and Judea, have their journey violently interrupted. They are rudely fixed to wood by nails and can move about no longer. His feet are literally lifted up from the earth so that not even his toes can touch the ground.

John has thought hard about this form of execution. He comes to see it as a parable, full of hidden meanings. Jesus is lifted up into the heart of God by his dying on the cross. Jesus continues his journey on Good Friday. He ceases to walk the paths of earth and marches up by means of that tree directly into the life of God.

But he travels upward not for himself alone. Just as a grain of wheat in its dying yields much fruit, just as the sun by mounting up into the heights each day draws upward the juices flowing in all plants and trees, so the lifting up of Jesus has the power to draw people, all people without exception, to himself. The coming of the Greeks (12:20-21) signaled the beginning of that mission of attraction.

Jesus cries out, inviting all people everywhere, Jews and Greeks alike, to move upward together in his company into the life of God.

FIRST LESSON: ISAIAH 49:1-6
LIGHT FOR THE NATIONS

Isaiah 49 opens on a note of confidence, as the servant articulates his sense of call. He was marked out for service from the moment of conception. The path he would travel was determined already when he was a mere kicking infant in his mother's womb. (See Jer. 1:5 and the words of Paul in Gal. 1:15 but especially the footwork of John the Baptist in Luke 1:41, 44.) The servant was named by God, and that means known and acknowledged from the first stirrings of life (cf. Matt. 1:21).

God gave to the servant a mouth like a sharp sword (cf. 50:4, Sunday), and God fashioned him to be an arrow piercing the hearts of listeners. The servant is God's secret weapon, and through him God will be glorified (Heb. 4:12; Eph. 6:17).

So the poem opens with pictures of intimacy between God and servant and with images of tasks to be accomplished. The servant speaks confidently at first, in rhetoric derived from the hunt and the military campaign. The servant begins to complain of laboring in vain and achieving nothing (see Isa. 6:5; John 12:37-43).

Nevertheless, the servant's first work among the tribes of Jacob was accepted by the Lord, and God sets the servant to a fresh task. Now the servant's work is to reach beyond Israel. God says, "I will give you as a light to the nations" (49:6). That task entails enormous difficulties, but the speed of light is always greater than the speed of darkness.

SECOND LESSON: 1 CORINTHIANS 1:18-31
THE WORD OF THE CROSS

Paul sums up the whole story about God and Jesus as "the word of the cross" (1:18). To outside observers the cross is nothing but foolishness and the most disgusting weakness. Even Corinthian Christians are happy to concentrate on Easter and leave the cross behind. For them the benefit of religion is access to God's power through the Spirit of the exalted Jesus. Paul believes that the Corinthians, by losing sight of the cross, are fundamentally altering their vision of God and of their journey under God.

Paul pictures the people of the world as moving along two disparate paths in two awesome processions. Some are in the process of "perishing," and others are in the process of "being saved" (1:18).

As Paul describes the choices people make and the paths they travel, it seems at first that he will heap scorn on "Jews and Gentiles" (1:23) or "Jews and Greeks" (1:22, 24). Those are colorful and comprehensive terms for all humanity. But it quickly becomes clear that Paul is really bearing down on the Corinthian Christians. Have these insiders themselves really taken to heart God's strange and cruciform wisdom? Do they cherish "the word of the cross"? Do they celebrate Easter but suffer amnesia about Good Friday? Paul worries that they set asunder what God has joined together. Christ's bursting forth from the tomb on Easter was a howling wind, but it did not uproot the tree of the cross. The resurrection set God's seal of approval on the way of the cross.

Paul sees God's wisdom as the key to the motley character of the Corinthian community. They are a patchwork quilt of the uneducated, the marginal, and the common. Not many of them could boast of the honor bestowed by school, by political assembly, or by birth in the bosom of a noble family (1:26-28). Yet they are "the saints of God" (1:2).

Then Paul further defines and defends God's strange wisdom by another argument (1:30-31). What is the source of any Corinthian's life? Whatever honors they may accord to Apollos or Cephas or Paul, perhaps because they were evangelized, catechized, or baptized by one of those great names, Christ Jesus alone is the fountain of their life with God. By the act of God, Christ Jesus and no other is our (a) righteousness, (b) sanctification, and (c) redemption.

This means that the Corinthians, thanks to the foolishness of the cross, (a) are at peace with God, (b) are no longer hopelessly mired in the ills of their society, and (c) have tasted sweet release from "the rulers of this world" and now enjoy freedom under God for joyous life. Apollos and Cephas and Paul have had a hand in all this, but only by preaching Christ Jesus and him crucified (2:2).

In Corinthian factions (1:10-16), each advertising itself as superior to the others, Paul sees a hankering after worldly power and wisdom. He smells a yearning for control over things and people, a desire to stand on top of the pyramid and look down.

Paul is heading in First Corinthians toward his great hymn on love (1 Corinthians 13). Here in our lesson he speaks of "the word of the cross," that shattering moment of the divine outpouring, the polar opposite of all lust for power over others.

Wednesday in Holy Week

Lutheran	Roman Catholic	Episcopal	Common Lectionary
Isa. 50:4-9a	Isa. 50:4-9	Isa. 50:4-9a	Isa. 50:4-9a
Rom. 5:6-11		Heb. 9:11-15, 24-28	Heb. 12:1-3
Matt. 26:14-25	Matt. 26:14-25	John 13:21-35 *or* Matt. 26:1-5, 14-25	John 13:21-30

(For the Old Testament lesson, see Palm Sunday.)

Egeria reports that on Wednesday night of Holy Week worshipers gather in front of the tomb of Jesus in the Anastasis. A presbyter reads aloud the narrative in which Judas Iscariot goes to the authorities and fixes a price for his betrayal of Jesus. When the people hear that passage, they begin to moan and groan aloud, and no one can help being moved to tears.

The Jerusalem lectionary of the early fifth century indicates that Matt. 26:3-16 was the appointed Gospel. Modern lectionaries differ concerning the reading, but they all agree with ancient custom that the theme for Wednesday is loyalty versus betrayal and that Judas can serve our meditation.

GOSPEL: MATTHEW 26:14-25
LOYALTY AND BETRAYAL

What exactly did Judas betray? Jesus' teachings, so that the authorities could be precise in their charges? That Jesus had been anointed, making a royal claim? Jesus' whereabouts, so he could be arrested in secret without raising a fuss? And what compelled Judas to such an act? His disappointment that Jesus was not the king he looked for? Did Judas hope to speed up the revolution by forcing Jesus to more dramatic action?

For whatever reason, Judas began to find the way of the Lord slippery and treacherous, dangerous to his own health and to the well-being of the people. He abandoned the path and turned on the Pathfinder. The way is not easy, and fog often obscures the landmarks. We may well feel sympathy for Judas.

Matthew, however, suggests that Judas was propelled simply by avarice: "How much will you give me?" (26:15). They agreed on thirty pieces of silver. Jesus has issued prior warnings in Matthew about the seductive power of money and about the impossibility of serving both God and mammon (6:19-21, 24; 19:22-23).

The first note concerning Judas (vv. 14-16) rounds off the priest's plot (vv. 3-5), and those two paragraphs together surround the report concerning the nameless woman who anointed Jesus' head (vv. 6-13). Judas and the priests thus stand in sharpest contrast with that woman. They are intent on killing Jesus, and money is the solid basis of their collusion. She honors Jesus with a costly gesture of devotion. They act in hopes of getting something. Her act is described as a "pouring out" (26:7, 12), in perfect harmony with the act of Jesus in "pouring out" his own blood (26:28).

The unnamed woman thus exhibits a deep understanding of the way Jesus travels, as she makes the same motions in her own life. Meanwhile, the priests and Judas, however they may have interpreted the path of Jesus, register only deadly opposition. (For further treatment, see the notes on Palm Sunday and on the parallel in John 12:1-11 on Monday.)

Unfortunately, by breaking off at v. 25, the lectionary stops short. Matthew has artfully arranged a set of parallels and contrasts in 26:20-35, so that Jesus casts a terrible light on Judas and on Peter. These two figures, Judas the traitor (21-25) and Peter the denier (30-35), surround Jesus as he speaks his words over bread and wine (26-29). Betrayal (Judas) and denial (Peter) are the grim framework within which Jesus acts and speaks.

The deeds and words of Jesus at that table, in brilliant contrast to treachery and cowardice, are all about fidelity. Jesus is faithful all the way to death, and his life, poured out in death, is a sacrifice initiating a covenant relationship, binding participants to one another and to their God with solemn promises and cords of love.

Instead of trying to probe the psyche of Judas in hopes of defining the character of his dis-ease about Jesus, Matthew invites meditation on the quality of our lives as pilgrim people. What does loyalty to Jesus, the great self-giver, entail? How many ways do we, as individuals and as communities, still betray and deny? How do our church buildings deny? Must our buildings and our programs repent and rise to new intimacy with God in Christ?

But the most urgent melody of all in the music of these texts is the insistence on God's own covenant love in Jesus Christ.

ALTERNATIVE GOSPEL: JOHN 13:21-30
BELOVED DISCIPLE

The identity of the Beloved Disciple is almost as elusive as that of the Isaianic servant. He seems to have been a real person, the founder of the Johannine community and guarantor of the tradition deposited in the Fourth Gospel. At the same time the Beloved Disciple has been idealized and serves as the model disciple. He is close to Jesus, quick to believe, perfect in trust, always following and never doubting, neither betraying nor denying, and for all these reasons he bears the clearest testimony. He embodies precisely those qualities and gifts that Jesus promised in his words concerning the coming Paraclete. In every imaginable way the Beloved Disciple contrasts with Judas, and, to a lesser extent, with Peter.

In all four Gospels, the story of Judas is told not so much out of curiosity about an individual disciple who has gone wrong as a warning to all who break bread with Jesus at his table. Will our feet walk the way of discipleship, or will we "lift the heel" against him? (13:18)? Will we cease to walk in the light (12:35) and break away from his table and company, plunging out into the night (13:30)? (Further reflections on this scene with Peter, Judas, and the Beloved Disciple are in the notes on Maundy Thursday.)

SECOND LESSON: ROMANS 5:6-11
BELOVED ENEMIES

In the opening paragraph of the chapter (5:1-5) Paul describes the present state of Christians: They have sailed into the snug harbor of God's grace, where they enjoy "peace with God through our Lord Jesus Christ." They lie at anchor in that harbor, but they have not quite yet reached home. Sharing in the glory of God still belongs to the future. Meanwhile two storms break around their heads, making them question whether they really are "acquitted" (justified) and at peace.

One is the storm of unspecified sufferings. But Paul says that God can use afflictions as a curriculum, schooling Christians in endurance and character and hope.

The second storm striking pilgrims is the awareness of their own sin. Does our sinfulness tell against our being the justified children of God? This is a serious question, and Paul takes it up in the lesson.

The whole point of 5:6-11 (and of Paul's message everywhere) is that God in Christ has intervened to meet people with divine grace not at their best, not at their moments of glittering goodness, not because they have made astonishing progress in the school of suffering and have developed moral and spiritual character.

On the contrary, while we could be described accurately as "helpless, ungodly, sinners, and enemies"—these are all Paul's words—Christ died for us. That death, that outpouring of blood, is the best definition of the heart of God. Paul's phrase "the justification of the ungodly" (Rom. 4:5) is the sharpest formulation of what he elsewhere styles "the word of the cross" (1 Cor. 1:18-31, Tuesday).

By virtue of God's costly love, Paul says, we are now justified and we will be saved. We are already, in the present, embraced by loving arms, at rest on the bosom of God (see John 13:23, one of today's Gospels). We are children of God, filled with the Spirit, crying "Abba" in spite of our suffering and sin.

Already embraced ("justified, at peace, reconciled"), we will be "saved" when the dear last day dawns and creation is liberated from bondage to decay (8:21). Neither things present nor things to come can separate us from the love of God in Christ Jesus (8:37-39).

ALTERNATIVE SECOND LESSON: HEBREWS 12:1-3
PILGRIMAGE AS RACING

This lesson picks up the tempo in picturing Christian existence not simply as a path to be walked but as a race to be run (cf. 1 Cor. 9:24; Gal. 2:2; 5:7; Phil. 2:16; 2 Tim. 4:7). In Greek, 12:1-2 is a single long sentence, and its main verb cries, "Let us run!"

The author summons Christians to a kind of Christic athleticism, calling them runners surrounded by a great "cloud of witnesses" (12:1). These witnesses are not mere spectators sunning themselves in the bleachers, passively watching while others sweat and compete. They are all those heroic competitors named in the immediately preceding paragraphs in the great recital of the ancient worthies: Abel, Enoch and Noah; Abraham, Sarah, Isaac, Jacob and Joseph; Moses and Rahab; judges, kings, prophets; women and men, all the way down to the Maccabean martyrs.

At the heart of that recitation, no fewer than eighteen lines are introduced with the phrase "by faith." Those eighteen sentences pound out the rhythm of the chapter like the beating of a drum, growing ever louder and more insistent.

In Hebrews, "faith" is the opposite of being attached to the things of earth, even such good things as the land of Israel, the city of Jerusalem, and the holy temple. All these are described as a passing shadow of the greater things to come.

Here in this world of visible, tangible, mutable things we have no abiding city (11:10; 12:22; 13:14). Faith understands that and looks away from all the passing glitter of earthbound reality. Faith grasps the reality of things hoped for and lives life as a disciplined race bound for the glory of God.

In Hebrews 11 the author urges readers to imitate the heroes of faith who ran the race before them. Now, in the climactic paragraph, the author calls readers to lift their eyes to Jesus, the great trailblazer. He raced as forerunner along the upward path and has now crossed the finish line, entering on our behalf into the heavenly sanctuary, moving beyond the world of striving and suffering into the world of perfection.

Hebrews speaks often of Jesus' death but only here names the cross as the instrument of his death. Jesus was contemptuous of the cross and did not allow it to swerve him from running his race.

Hebrews avoids calling people to take up their cross, but this work does summon Christians to run their own race behind the one who moved to the cross and by means of it to God's right hand.

What impedes them in their race? Persecution belongs to their past. In the present they seem to be threatened not so much by hostile neighbors as by a kind of weariness, a loss of focus, the onset of lethargy.

HOLY PLACE AS WITNESS

For Cyril and Egeria, unlike the author of Hebrews, the earthly realities are not mere shadows but are powerful witnesses to the truth of God in Jesus Christ.

Cyril in his lectures to catechumens (10.19) points to many witnesses: God, the Holy Spirit, and the archangel Gabriel; Anna, Simeon, and John the Baptist. But then Cyril calls the roll of geographical realities. He loves to call the land itself and especially sites in and around Jerusalem as witnesses.

We can see him point as he speaks: "Golgotha the holy hill standing above us here"; "the holy wood of the cross seen among us to this day"; "the Holy Tomb and the stone which lies there to this day." All these are not mute but speak eloquently of what God has done in Christ.

Egeria's one constant companion in all her travels is her Bible. It testifies to the holiness of the topography over which she treads, and she finds confirmation of the truth of Scripture written in the hills and valleys she visits.

Scripture and holy places together with monks and bishops and Christian women and men were all part of "the cloud of witnesses" surrounding Egeria and Cyril.

It may seem like a great leap from Egeria to Mark Twain, who visited Jerusalem in the summer of 1867. *Innocents Abroad,* an irreverent account of his journey from new world to old, carries the subtitle *New Pilgrims' Progress.* In it he pokes fun at everything—his fellow travelers, the inhabitants of Paris and Rome and their cultured pretensions, the superstitions of the holy land. But he can be serious.

He spent his first evening in Jerusalem simply trying to comprehend the fact that he was actually in the city "where Solomon dwelt, where Abraham held converse with the Deity, where walls still stand that witnessed the spectacle of the crucifixion" (p. 444).

Amid the buildings, shrines, relics, and ruins of Jerusalem, the Church of the Holy Sepulchre gained the strongest hold on his imagination. He called it "the most illustrious edifice in Christendom" (p. 457). Weary of everything else, he returned to it every day. He was scandalized by its tawdry ornamentation, its primitive rituals, its smoke and gloom, its legends and superstitions.

He saw the place where Adam and Melchizedek were buried, where Jesus was whipped and imprisoned, where Mary Magdalene and John stood beneath the cross, where the crown of thorns and true cross were discovered, where the angel sat on Easter morning. And he scoffed at all those "witnesses."

The place of crucifixion, however, affected him differently. It cast its spell on him: "I looked upon the place where the true cross once stood, with a far more absorbing interest than I had ever felt in any earthly thing before" (p. 456).

In the Church of the Holy Sepulchre, he said he struggled to remember that "Christ was not crucified in a church. . . . The great event transpired in the open air, and not in a gloomy, candle-lighted cell in a little corner of a vast church, upstairs—a small cell all bejeweled and bespangled with flashy ornamentation, in execrable taste" (p. 456).

He thought at last of the varied brands of "loyalty" Christians have displayed toward this church and the one it honors. Pilgrims streaming from earth's remotest regions shed their tears here. But gallant knights also came and shed rivers of blood here, and they did it out of respect for the Prince of Peace. What is "loyalty" to the Christ?

John Bunyan, in issuing the second part of his *Pilgrim's Progress* (1684), reflected on the fact that part one had been published in several languages. He wrote a satiric poem including these two lines: "In France and Flanders where men kill each other, / My pilgrim is esteemed a friend, a brother."

Wednesday of Holy Week is an apt time to reflect on varied human responses to the love of God.

Maundy Thursday

Lutheran	Roman Catholic	Episcopal	Common Lectionary
Exod. 12:1-14	Exod. 12:1-8, 11-14	Exod. 12:1-14a	Exod. 12:1-14
1 Cor. 11:17-32	1 Cor. 11:23-26	1 Cor. 11:23-26	1 Cor. 11:23-26
John 13:1-17, 34	John 13:1-15	John 13:1-15	John 13:1-15

Egeria reports that on this one day of the year the worshipers receive communion in the space she calls Behind the Cross. The congregation crowds as close as possible to Golgotha, to which they have access at the head of the southernmost aisle of Constantine's basilica (the Martyrium).

They do not go out to Mount Zion and locate their service there in "the upper room" in a dramatic reenactment of the first Holy Thursday. (They would begin to do that shortly after Egeria's time.) Instead, reports Egeria, they draw near to the cross of the living Christ. That is exactly how John and Paul understand the church's supper.

Egeria says nothing about footwashing. When that custom first arose, it was practiced in connection with baptisms, signifying purification from sin and the gift of salvation. By the seventh century footwashing had come to be a separate ritual of Maundy Thursday. The hymn "Ubi Caritas" ("Where charity and love abound, There precisely God is found") was composed around the year 800 as a Maundy Thursday meditation on the footwashing.

Since the middle of the fifth century it has been customary on this day to prepare the oil that will be used throughout the year for baptisms, confirmations, ordinations, and the anointing of the sick. In the past generation Maundy Thursday in some parts of the Roman Catholic, Episcopal, and Lutheran communions has been selected as a day for services devoted to the renewal of priestly vows.

GOSPEL: JOHN 13:1-17, 34
WASHING THEIR FEET

The first four verses (13:1-4) are a poignant introduction both to this entire new section of the Gospel and to the footwashing that immediately follows. John heaps up phrases like the mournful tolling of some great bell, so there can be no mistaking the supreme solemnity of the act to follow.

It is Passover time, with its feasting on slaughtered lambs. Now at last is "the hour" (2:4; 7:30) for Jesus to "move out from this world," passing over not to dust and ashes but to "the Father" from whom he has come forth.

Jesus has always loved "his own" (cf. 1:11), and now he will (at the cross) fully and finally enact the great love he has for them (13:1).

During dinner (13:2), and readers know this is his last earthly dinner, Jesus prepares himself like an athlete for his ultimate contest with his archrival, the devil.

His equipment for the struggle is "knowledge" that his historical path is backed by the full authority of God and that God is both the alpha and the omega of his journey. Because he moves knowingly, he neither wanders nor leads astray (13:3).

Jesus lays aside his outer garment, mirroring the gesture of the good shepherd who lays aside his life (10:17-18). And he binds himself with a towel. Elsewhere he says Peter will one day be "bound" by enemies and be taken under alien control (21:18). Jesus, however, is not forced by others to travel the way of the cross. He freely readies himself for the great task at hand (13:4).

Only after elaborate preparation does he pour water into a bowl and begin to wash his disciples' feet (13:5). The whole paragraph builds steadily to this strange washing. It stands here at the start of the Book of Glory, and readers are compelled to contemplate that washing as they approach the cross and empty tomb. So rich and mysterious is this washing that John offers not one but two separate interpretations of it (one in vv. 6-10 and a second in 11-20).

At first Peter recoils in disgust and confusion. He honors Jesus too highly to accept such slavish ministrations at Jesus' hands. His universe is shattered if the greater washes the feet of the lesser. He cries out in defense of his old world, with its customary and comfortable hierarchies. He is incapable of interpreting the dignity of Jesus in terms of service.

In response to Peter, Jesus makes the astonishing declaration that this washing is absolutely indispensable. It is no mere polite gesture, like the washings offered by slaves to guests appearing at the home of their host. Anyone lacking the washing that Jesus offers will be cut off and have no share in his company, and that means no sharing in the life of God. Shifting gears, Peter then begs Jesus to wash his face and his hands also. Unnecessary, says Jesus. Once a person has received the bath he offers, there is no need for any further washing.

What washing can this possibly be? What washing is such a powerful necessity? What washing falls upon the world like Noah's flood, carrying away everything old so that a new world emerges clean and fresh? Baptism is the answer most frequently given, but the whole introduction (13:1-5) leads rather to the conclusion that Jesus' outpoured life is itself the crucial bath. The totality of his life, from beginning to goal at the cross, is summed up as agape (13:1). Without the "service" of that purifying love, how can people be rescued from their lostness and gathered for life (3:16)?

With this washing we stand at the threshold of the farewell discourse. At its end Jesus will speak in prayer about his disciples as people "sanctified" by the word and by truth (17:17-19). "Sanctified" means separated from everything false and hateful. It means being brought fully into the sphere of divine life. The sanctifying word of truth is Jesus himself, who came forth from God and is coursing upward again into the heart of God by means of the love that carries him to the cross.

That washing, which Peter instinctively found so repulsive, is nothing less than the cleansing flood of God's agape pouring with tidal force through Jesus' life and death (cf. 1 John 1:7, 9).

The second interpreting paragraph (11-20) declares in more pedestrian fashion that the footwashing serves as an example of humility and is to be imitated by all disciples. In that ancient culture merely touching someone's feet meant displaying obsequious politeness to a person of prestige and power (cf. John 12:1-11, Monday; Matt. 28:9 in the final reading of the Easter Vigil). Washing feet was the work of slaves. John the Baptist declared that he was such an unworthy person that he was not fit even to untie the sandals of the coming one (John 1:27; cf. 1 Sam. 25:41).

By stripping for action and washing his disciples' feet, Jesus assigns revolutionary definitions to the old words "teacher" (*didaskalos*) and "master" (*kyrios*) and summons his disciples to introduce the new lexicography into the syntax of all their relationships.

13:21-30. By washing his disciples' feet, Jesus provokes a confused chorus of responses in the inner circle. The evangelist quickly sketches the reactions of three of those whom Jesus cleansed: Peter, Judas, and the Beloved Disciple.

Peter still falls short of comprehending the path that Jesus travels and is full of questions about Jesus' way. Judas swerves off that path and exits into the night of his lostness. The Beloved Disciple reclines on Jesus' breast, in an attitude that speaks at once of intimacy and acceptance. He rests secure and serene on the one who is himself "the real and living way" (John 14:6). (For further notes see Wednesday.)

13:31-38. This paragraph, marking the transition to the farewell discourse proper, contains the final sentence (v. 34) of the Gospel selection. This verse speaks of the "new commandment" of agape, and that *mandatum novum* gives this day its name: "Maundy" Thursday (cf. John 15:12-17; 1 John 3:23; 2 John 5). Jesus summons disciples, washed by love, to become rivers of love in all their dealings with others (cf. 7:38-39).

SECOND LESSON: 1 CORINTHIANS 11:23-26
PROCLAIM THE LORD'S LOVING DEATH

The Eucharist at Corinth had degenerated into something resembling a bacchanalian revel. Wine flowed abundantly as a means of inducing ecstasy. Loss of ego control made room for heavenly powers to take over one's consciousness. Divine life rushed in with intoxicating force. Bursting with spiritual energy, worshipers were caught up to heaven in a rush of self-transcendence.

But Paul summons the Corinthians back to earth, back to the neighbor (even the lowest members of the body), and back to the agape-filled cross of Jesus Christ. Paul's summons takes the form of a recitation of the "words of institution" (or "words of interpretation"), with his own commentary on those words.

In effect, Paul asks, "What is the source of the words of our tradition?" He reminds the Corinthians that the words were first spoken not in broad daylight but "in the night," the time for dark deeds. In that night the Lord Jesus "was handed over," betrayed by one of the inner circle, victim of treachery not at the hands of some stranger but stricken by one of his own (11:23).

What did Jesus do as he spoke the words of our celebration? He did not merely recite the words and then fill his mouth with bread and his belly with wine. He "broke" the bread and called that fractured food his body, and his broken body was far more than his own private tragedy. He called it food yielded up "for you" (11:24).

The cup he took that night was no intoxicating potion, no vessel of escape. It was (and is) the signal of a fresh community-building covenant in his "blood," his very real and really violent death (11:25).

This meal is the church's eternal proclamation of his agapeic living and dying (11:26). Celebration of this meal erects the cross in the center of the community. The meal is an act of remembrance (11:24, 25), sharply focused on the past breaking of his body and the historic outpouring of his life at the cross (cf. 1 Cor. 1:18-31, Tuesday of Holy Week).

At the same time, this meal is celebrated in hope. Participants cry out for the cosmic triumph of the one who has already loved them to the uttermost (1 Cor. 16:22). Paul invites the Corinthians to gorge themselves not on wine but on love (1 Corinthians 13) as they continue their pilgrimage between the cross and the coming final triumph of the Lord.

FIRST LESSON: EXODUS 12:1-14
OUT OF EGYPT

As Paul addresses the Corinthians in chapters 10 and 11, he admits that he has been meditating on the early history of Israel. He has been contemplating the gifts of God and the odd responses of the people of God as they walk their hazardous path through the world.

The Exodus account of the institution of the Passover speaks of moving on life's journey sustained by memory and hope, just like Paul's recitation of the institution of the Lord's meal. Passover and the Lord's Supper both fix the imagination on founding events and on transcendent goals. Without them we are in danger of wandering aimlessly in the wilderness of life, victims of amnesia or despair.

Both the church's Lord Supper and Israel's Passover are full of pathos. Both are rituals of violence and blood, of mortal danger and heaven's rescuing hand. Both are food for hard journeys in the wilderness.

Exodus 12 is partly a description of the first Passover and partly a set of rubrics for the annual celebration. This meal they shall celebrate not once but every year, because the life of freedom under God and with God is always a journey, always an adventure, always movement toward promise.

From the beginning, Passover has been a household meal celebrated not at tabernacle or temple but in homes (Exod. 12:3-4). The blood of freshly slaughtered lambs was painted on the doorposts and lintels of their houses (12:5-7). The lamb was roasted and its flesh entirely consumed by family and neighbors (12:8-10).

The instructions for eating the lamb and the unleavened bread are instructions for living all of life: with loins girded (cf. John 13:4), with sandals on the feet, and with staff in hand. And eat the Passover in haste, because it is prologue to escape (Exod. 12:11).

This meal bids farewell to easy living. It is a gearing up for serious travel. It speaks to the banqueters of a journey through wild places and perils unknown, leading by unfamiliar paths to a land of promise as yet unseen.

At times people experience life as a trackless waste or a barren landscape. Individuals and whole nations appear to be at sea or hopelessly lost. The Exodus and the Lord's Supper are not detailed maps solving all life's problems in advance. But they do tell a story at once bracing and challenging, coherent and compelling. They show us a set of footprints moving out toward the horizon, and they call us to follow.

Good Friday

Lutheran	Roman Catholic	Episcopal	Common Lectionary
Isa. 52:13—53:12	Isa. 52:13—53:12	Isa. 52:13—53:12	Isa. 52:13—53:12
Heb. 4:14-16; 5:7-9	Heb. 4:14-16; 5:7-9	Heb. 10:1-25	Heb. 4:14-16; 5:7-9
John 18:1—19:42 or John 19:17-30	John 18:1—19:42	John 19:1-37	John 18:1—19:42 or John 19:17-30

Egeria reports that on Friday morning of Great Week in Jerusalem, a table is placed at Golgotha in the chapel called Behind the Cross (see introduction to Maundy Thursday). The bishop sits at the table flanked by watchful deacons. On the table is a gold and silver vessel containing the holy wood of the cross and also the title inscribed by Pilate. The wood and the title are removed from the box and laid on the table for viewing and adoration. From eight in the morning until noon, all the people, both catechumens and the faithful, approach in a single file. At the table they bow, touching the wood first with their forehead and then with their eyes. They kiss it. No one stretches out a hand to touch it.

On one occasion, Egeria says, an overzealous worshiper bit off a piece of the holy wood and stole it away in his teeth. Since that time deacons have stood guard with the bishop at the table.

At noon the people gather in the courtyard between Golgotha and the Anastasis. Various Scriptures describing the sufferings of Jesus are read: psalms and epistles and selections from Acts. When three o'clock arrives, the Passion according to Saint John is read.

For centuries Good Friday has been a day for venerating the cross and meditating on Jesus' path to the cross. Kissing the cross and biting the cross may seem primitive or beside the point. But if we do not venerate the cross, then what do we adore? What symbols and icons move us?

No doubt the adoration of the cross can degenerate into something maudlin or superstitious. It may reinforce unhealthy feelings of inferiority, passivity, self-pity, or victimhood. But it may also suggest a celebration of the triumph of the crucified, of the one who lived and loved with a passion, who would not be moved from his path by the threats of politicians, the arguments of clergy, or the vacillations of his own disciples. The cross is a sign of immense and awesome strength: the strength of love, of protest, of hope.

Near Saiuliai in Lithuania a small hill covered with crosses rises from surrounding grain fields. On that hill in 1863 cossacks buried a chapel together with its Lithuanian occupants. Since that time the hill has been the Golgotha of Lithuania and a goal of pilgrimage.

At one time three thousand crosses, handcrafted of wood and metal in traditional Lithuanian styles, stood on the hill. During the years of communist domination, the crosses were repeatedly pulled up and thrown into the river, sawn in two and burned ("sent to heaven in smoke"), or trucked off and used as boards in government building projects. But crosses kept on appearing, erected as acts of piety and political protest.

In 1970 Father Algirdas Mocius completed a barefoot walk of forty miles carrying a wooden cross. He set it up on the hill on Holy Cross Day, September 14.

In Egeria's time, at the end of the fourth century, September 14 was celebrated with adoration of the cross, just as on Good Friday. September 14 was a double holiday. The Church of the Holy Sepulchre had been dedicated on September 14, 335, and the discovery of the true cross had also come to be celebrated on September 14. Constantine's mother, Helena, had discovered the cross, according to Ambrose of Milan, writing in 395 (eleven years after Egeria's sojourn in Jerusalem).

Around 401 the theologian Rufinus described a test that was devised to determine which of the crosses Helena discovered had belonged to Jesus. Bishop Macarius (bishop of Jerusalem in the Nicene era) knew a woman in the neighborhood who was on the verge of death. Each cross was brought to her. She touched two of them without recovering. When she touched the third, she was cured instantly. It was judged to be the true cross of Jesus.

How shall we speak of the healing power of the cross, of God's love, of Christ's love, in our lives? If love given and love received is not healing, then what is?

GOSPEL: JOHN 18:1—19:42
FRIDAY OF GLORY

Jesus' journey to the cross is a triumphal procession to coronation and glory. Others may read it as a terrifying journey to the heart of darkness, but John reads it as Jesus' pilgrimage into the blinding light of the heart of God.

From Dining Room to Garden (18:1-11)

Jesus leaves the banquet room and takes the path to a mysterious "garden." The Synoptic Gospels never mention a garden. They speak simply of "Gethsemane" on the slopes of the Mount of Olives (cf. Mark 14:26, 32 and parallels). John never uses the name Gethsemane but quietly introduces word of a "garden" (18:1; cf. 19:41; 20:15).

What "garden" is this? John opens his Gospel (1:1) with echoes of Genesis: "In the beginning." By speaking of a garden, John signals once again that God is fashioning a new humanity in this Jesus.

On one level the capture and crucifixion of Jesus are deeds of evil committed under cover of darkness. But on the level of deeper reality, his arrest and death mark the dawn of the light of the new creation. John sees a new Eden in this strange "garden" outside Jerusalem beyond the Kidron watercourse.

Judas knew the place and came now not as disciple but as traitor. John paints an astonishing scene, so odd that translations and commentaries cannot believe it and spare no effort to tone it down and render it more plausible.

John says that Judas came out to the garden at the head of what the RSV calls a *band* of Roman soldiers. The NRSV changes the word to *detachment*. John uses the Greek word *speira,* which means literally a military unit of six hundred soldiers. That is not all. They came with assorted "police," probably those particular Levites whose tasks included crowd control in the temple precincts.

So Judas came out leading six hundred Roman soldiers plus assorted Jewish police. That many? Unbelievable! So we adopt various strategies to whittle down that preposterous number. The very vagueness of the words *band* and *detachment* have commended them to translators.

But the Gospels (John least of all) did not regard the power of God as something easy to calculate and believe. And power is the issue here. What power is capable of generating and sustaining genuine human life? What power can beat back the darkness and undo the mischief of the fall? Are the powers represented by Pilate's soldiers or temple police capable of it?

During that fateful Passover season, both Pilate and Jesus had led processions into Jerusalem. Here a few nights later the representatives of Roman power march out from the city across the Kidron to confront Jesus in the garden. Can they seize him and discredit his claims? Can they themselves lead humanity to a new Eden?

John's account drips with irony. Six hundred soldiers together with an unspecified number of police come marching out. They approach the garden in total ignorance concerning the one who is the light of the world (8:12; 9:5), and so they all carry "lanterns and torches and weapons." In their journey through life they rely for guidance and protection on poor artificial lights and on power flowing from weapons forged of iron.

Jesus steps forward, asking that fundamental question, "Whom do you seek?" (cf. 1:38; 20:15). In the harsh contrasts of the Fourth Gospel, people seek Jesus only because they wish to dwell in God through Christ or because they desire to kill Jesus.

They name their quarry, and Jesus responds, "I am." As soon as he uttered those two words, "I am," John says that "they all fell back onto the ground." It pays to slow down our reading and to picture the scene literally as John reports it. Think of all six hundred (plus!). If they walked to the garden in single file, the line would have stretched nearly half a mile. John says that all of them with their torches and weapons fell on their backs to the ground! The scene is both comical and deadly serious. Those who walk in the darkness will always stumble (11:10; 12:35).

Continue to read as literally as possible. The six hundred-plus fell to the ground, and the text does not say that they got up. Picture them all stretched out on the ground as the action goes on.

Jesus repeats his question: "Whom do you seek?" Again they respond, "Jesus the Nazarene." Once more he identifies himself: "I am." Not "I am Jesus" or "I am the one you are seeking" or even "I am he." But simply and mysteriously, "I am" (cf. 8:58).

The divine presence is welling up in Jesus. Holy energy bursts forth, not to slit the throats of his enemies or to set his friends on thrones. He does, however, serve his friends. Jesus cuts a curious deal on their behalf: "If you let these disciples go on their way, I will let you seize me," he says. "My life for theirs!"

Jesus gives himself up, and he does so on behalf of others. That he died for the many is stated everywhere in the New Testament in dozens of ways. John here paints the great exchange in broad, almost comic, strokes.

The comedy continues. Jesus looms over his enemies and absolutely dominates the scene. At that precise moment, in a fit of monumental misunderstanding, Peter draws his sword!

What can Peter be thinking? That Jesus needs protecting? This Jesus who has just bowled over more than six hundred armed men by speaking two words? Swinging his sword in reliance on sharp iron, Peter proceeds to cut off the ear of Malchus. And then what? Was Peter going to walk down the whole long file of fallen soldiers and cut off every ear? He is a tragicomic figure representing the long line of those Christians who have enormous difficulty coming to terms with Jesus as a Lord who has renounced the sword and with God who will not use power the way we desire.

Peter's act reveals one of God's great problems. God has effectively intruded into our space and time in Jesus. Yet for all his authority over water and bread, over sickbed and tomb, the Son of God is not omnipotent in dealing with human beings. They persist in the awful freedom to ignore him or misjudge him, just like Peter.

From Garden to Palace (18:12-27)

(On the trial, see also Matt. 26:57-75, Palm/Passion Sunday)

Jesus permits the soldiers and police to tie his hands and lead him to Annas, powerful member of the high priestly circle (18:12-14). Peter and "another disciple" (almost certainly the Beloved Disciple) follow behind and, by turns, enter the courtyard, where Peter at a charcoal fire (21:9) utters his first denial (18:15-18).

By having Annas question Jesus about "his disciples and his teaching," John in effect asks readers to pass in review all the words and deeds of Jesus recorded in the preceding chapters. What is it about that teaching that so disturbs the wise and powerful of this world, not to mention all of us who hanker after power over others or after wisdoms and truths that give us mastery, control, and security (18:19-24)? Peter denies Jesus for a second and third time (21:15-17).

Back and Forth (18:28—19:16)

In earlier chapters of John, talk about "the sovereignty of God" is rare (except 3:3, 5). Ordinarily in John's Gospel talk revolves instead around "life eternal" (cf. 3:16). But here in the conversation between Pilate and Jesus, talk about king and kingship or sovereignty dominates the seven paragraphs. Is Jesus a king? Does he wield power? If so, what are his politics?

The material is carefully arranged. Four scenes "outside" (18:28-32, 38b-40; 19:4-7, 12-16) alternate with three scenes "inside" the Praetorium (18:33-38a; 19:1-3, 8-11). Pilate (taking Jesus with him) keeps moving in and out. Outside Pilate speaks to the crowd; inside he speaks privately with Jesus.

Why all this movement in and out, back and forth? From one angle, Pilate looks like the astute negotiator, practicing shuttle diplomacy, giving the appearance of patience as he moves between opposing parties. Or is Pilate the picture of an anguished human being, compelled to make a hard choice between God and the world and hating every minute of it? Or is Pilate the cagey survivor, traveling a zigzag course, a crooked path between opposing points of view, always sniffing out a way to save his own skin?

Pilate is conducting a trial, but finally he himself is on trial. He makes an effort to dispense that famous Roman justice, and at first he seems to be even an advocate of Jesus. But gradually he buckles under pressure (19:12) and ultimately yields to the clamorings of the crowd.

Jesus' priestly enemies are fixated on correctness. At the beginning they scrupulously refrain from entering the Roman headquarters building, since contact with the gentile dwelling would render them ceremonially unclean (18:28). Jesus' accusers carefully maintain their ritual purity so that they may later that night eat the Passover meal and celebrate their being set apart as God's holy people. But at the end of the section (19:15) they utter that terrible self-denunciation: "We have no king but Caesar."

The central scene in the series of seven comes in 19:1-3, when Roman soldiers taunt Jesus with a mock enthronement. They weave a crown out of spiky thorns and shove it on his head. They drape his shoulders with a purple robe (to denote royalty). Then they take turns saluting him as "king of the Jews."

Readers catch the irony. They know that unwittingly the soldiers are enacting the truth. Jesus really is the irruption of God's sovereign majesty in our midst. Readers may even enjoy Pilate's discomfiture or the priest's duplicity.

But through this trial John is pressing questions on the readers. They are under scrutiny. Do readers acknowledge God above the gods of flag and nation, race and religion? John asks whether readers recognize

God's sovereign claims on them, or do they too declare, "We have no king but Caesar" (19:15)?

The trial ends, and Pilate hands Jesus over to crucifixion. Nothing is said of stripping Jesus of his royal regalia. So he goes to the cross wearing the crown and the royal robe.

Up to the Cross and Glory (19:17-30)

The crucifixion in John's Gospel lacks details familiar from the Synoptics. On the way to the cross, Jesus requires no Simon of Cyrene. He is mounting powerfully to his throne and carries his cross "by himself" (19:17). John reports no darkness over all the earth from noon till three. In John's Gospel the crucifixion is Jesus' most brilliant hour, the moment when he comes into his own as light of the world (8:12; 9:5). The glory of his cross banishes darkness by its mystic glow, casting a sometimes harsh light on the realities of human institutions of holiness and power (cf. 3:19-21).

Once Jesus is lifted up onto the cross, no one mocks him—not soldiers, not high priests and elders, not passersby, and not his fellow crucified. He is Mighty Victim, and no weeping women mourn or pity him. Jesus utters no cry of forsakenness in this Gospel, because at the cross he is entering once more into God's own glory.

In John's passion narrative humans do not mock, women do not weep, nature does not mourn, and God does not abandon Jesus. His crucifixion is his elevation to a throne high and exalted above every earthly throne.

Pilate testifies to the truth of Jesus' enthronement. John slows the pace of the narrative to compel readers to contemplate the title King of the Jews. It was inscribed in three tongues. Hebrew, Greek, and Latin were the languages of religion, culture, and government. Priests raised a protest over that triply engraved proclamation, but Pilate uttered his famous defense. And if Pilate's enscripturated message stands, how much more will sacred Scripture stand.

As king installed on his throne, Jesus dispenses favors and hears cases. That is the meaning of the following scenes.

1. In describing the disposition of Jesus' garments (19:23-24), John has not misunderstood poetic parallelism. He sees an opportunity in the words of the psalm. He plays with the words in deliberately lit-eralistic fashion, finding in them an opening for one of his great themes.

Philo thought that the seamless robe of the Jewish high priest signified the sublime Logos, the sweet wisdom of God, which sustains the universe and makes it hang together. Jesus' robe was seamless and whole, not cut or torn asunder at his dying. It symbolizes the gift of oneness he bestows. That robe and that gift of union with God could come into the possession of others only by Jesus' dying. Exactly by not clinging selfishly to life but by yielding up his life, this king on the cross bestows the blessing of oneness with God (10:16; 11:52; 17:11).

2. At the cross Jesus creates new human community. He addresses his Beloved Disciple and his mother: "Behold your mother! Behold your son!" (19:25-27). His dying love crosses boundaries, binding heart to heart in a new human family.

A robe and a family: His dying bequeaths a fresh and undivided oneness, a new community between heaven and earth, and a new family upon the earth.

3. From his throne he reigns, calling on soldiers like a king ordering his servants: "Bring me my royal cup, for I thirst!" This cup is neither mockery nor pity, as in the Synoptic Gospels. Nor does Jesus physically need this drink. He calls for it, says the evangelist, only in order to fulfill Scripture down to the last detail. His dying, because it is the climax of a perfect love (13:1), fulfills Scripture and the will of God. His goal (*telos*) achieved, he cries, "It is finished" (*tetelestai*, 19:28-30).

From Cross to Garden (19:31-42)

The executions are hurried along so that the holy day might not be profaned (cf. 18:28). But Jesus has given up his life freely and does not need to have it wrenched from him by any further torture (10:18). Therefore, John (alone) tells us, his bones are not broken. In the unbroken wholeness of Jesus' triumphant body the author finds a testimony to God's invincible care for the righteous (Ps. 34:20). Readers once more contemplate a sign of unsplintered oneness and integrity (cf. 19:23-27).

Soldiers lance Jesus' side near his giant heart, and out pour "blood and water" or "a flow of blood" or even "blood flowing like a river." Blood means life. His enemies had planned his death in order to defeat his life and dam its flow. But precisely by means of his dying the floodgates are burst, and his life begins to pour out into the universe with healing power (cf. 7:38).

John paints scenes of mythic proportions with broad strokes of his pen. Jesus' burial at the hands of Joseph and Nicodemus surpasses extravagance. The precious mixture they assemble weighs one hundred pounds (Roman, the equivalent of seventy-five pounds American). The few ounces poured on his feet by Mary at Bethany (John 12:1-11, Monday) equaled in value the total annual income of a day laborer. Joseph and Nicodemus complete the funeral of Jesus in a manner fit for a king (see the burial of King Asa in 2 Chron. 16:14).

John concludes his account by speaking twice in rapid succession of a "garden" and by connecting that garden as intimately as possible with both the cross and the tomb (19:41-42). Thus he mentions a garden at both the beginning (18:1) and the end of the passion narrative (cf. 20:15).

In the death and resurrection of Jesus, the way to Eden has been opened up. The angel and the flaming sword cease their sentry duty, the mist burns off, and the path becomes clear. Humankind is no longer condemned to aimless wandering in the land of Nod, east of Eden.

TOMBS AND HOLY PLACES

The tombs of saints have always been seen as peculiarly charged places. This seems odd, since tombs are signs of weakness, and corpses contaminate. But the tombs of saints and martyrs hold in their embrace the mortal remains of those whom the world killed but of whom God approves. Their tombs are signs of the struggle between God and world. They are in some sense outposts of heaven, places where pilgrims come into contact with God and come under God's protection while signaling their willingness to stand in opposition to the world.

From the beginning, the tomb of Jesus was seen as a place to tap the power of heaven and to learn how to be prophetic and counter-cultural. The tomb of Jesus of course was empty, but he had used that tomb. He had really died and had been buried. Strange new light and life arose precisely there in a place of death and darkness and defeat. God wrote new definitions of holiness and power in the cross and empty tomb of Jesus.

Jerome was a frequent visitor to the tomb. Like John, Jerome saw in that tomb in the garden a new Eden. Like the author of Hebrews (see below), Jerome contemplated the tomb from a cultic angle and confessed that he venerated the Lord's sepulchre just as ancient Israel venerated the Holy of Holies (Letter 46.5).

SECOND LESSON: HEBREWS 4:14-16; 5:7-9; 10:1-25

What is the cross? Citizens and subjects of the Roman Empire saw it as dread engine of destruction. It spelled shameful ruin for criminals and slaves.

Jesus suffered execution on the hard wood of Golgotha's cross. Sinking down, he was embraced by the stone-cold tomb. To the casual eye, Jesus' Good Friday journey looks like the universal human passage from life to death, from breath to burial, earth returning to earth, except that he went down under the earth in terrible fashion.

Through profound meditation, early Christians came to see the death of Jesus and their own lives in a revolutionary light. Apostles and evangelists ransacked the treasury of biblical tradition and the depths of human experience, searching for images potent enough to articulate their convictions concerning the path Jesus traveled on Good Friday.

At the cross he not only poured out his life but sent streaming a mighty flood of charity (John 13:1) and forgiveness (Luke 23:34; Matt. 26:28). His dying ransomed captives from fearful bondage (Mark 10:45). Good Friday was the hour of his glorious coronation and the beginning of God's seizure of power in a wayward creation (John). The cross is the power of God and the wisdom of God (1 Corinthians).

The author of Hebrews gazed steadily at the cross, that brutal instrument of torture, and began to see that the hand of God had touched and transfigured it. The cross is a great wooden staircase stretching all the way from earth to highest heaven. On Good Friday's cross Jesus mounted up as final High Priest and "passed through the heavens" into the presence of God (4:14).

The most frequently quoted piece of Scripture in the New Testament is Psalm 110:1, "The Lord [God] said to my Lord [Messiah], 'Sit at my right hand.' " The author of Hebrews read beyond that verse down to v. 4 and was arrested by the declaration "You [Lord-Messiah] are a priest forever" drawn not from the ranks of Levites but "after the order of Melchizedek."

Intrigued by cultic images, the author envisioned the entire ministry of Jesus, culminating on Good Friday, as a single sustained priestly offering of obedience. Images of sacrifice and journey overlapped in the author's mind. The way of Jesus was like the pilgrimage of Abraham and Sarah (11:8-16), like the wilderness march of Israel under Moses and Joshua (3:1—4:10).

But in the lessons for Good Friday (4:14-16; 5:7-9; and 10:1-25), and in the whole central section of Hebrews, we see the author's energy consumed by parallels between the path of Jesus and the restless movements of priests at the sanctuary.

Carrying offerings in sanctified hands, priests journeyed day by day into the holy place, in and out, back and forth, in ceaseless motion, never finishing, never finding rest. Once every year, the high priest went behind the curtain into the Holy of Holies, performed the prescribed ritual, and departed only to return the following year and the year after that, never achieving the goal.

On Good Friday Jesus completed his pilgrimage by climbing the cross to the celestial Holy of Holies. He offered a single sacrifice for sin, effective for all time, touching the conscience and not the body only. Having finished his work, he "stands" no longer. Both standing and moving were to the author infallible signs of unfinished work. Jesus now "sits" exactly as Psalm 110:4 says. He sits because his work of linking earth and heaven is gloriously accomplished (10:12).

Jesus did not simply cross the line separating the land of the Chaldees from the land of Canaan, or cross boundaries like the Red Sea, the wilderness, and the Jordan River, or step from profane court to holy place and then past the curtain into the Holy of Holies. The real and terrible rending of his flesh on Good Friday means that he has pierced all the circling heavenly spheres and penetrated into God's own inner sanctum. At his dying he stepped across the great unbridgeable gulf and entered God's throne room.

His obedience bridges the gulf. Mercy is enthroned. Compassion reigns on high. "Let us draw near."

FIRST LESSON: ISAIAH 52:13—53:12

Words of God at beginning (52:13-15) and end (53:11b-12) surround words of astonished human beings (53:1-11a).

52:13-15. God cries, "Look! My servant will prosper." In language echoed by the fourth evangelist, God says the servant "will be exalted and lifted up." In view of the servant's terrible humiliation, his exaltation is almost unbelievable.

53:1-11a. His biography is a story of pain and rejection: In his first days he was like a plant sprouting in dry, hostile ground (53:2). In his middle days he was "a man of sorrows" (53:3) traveling a path of sorrows (via dolorosa). In the end he was unjustly condemned and executed, and his martyred body was dumped without ceremony into the grave (53:8-9).

But the grief and sorrows gathered like clouds around his head are not his own. They are our griefs and our sorrows. He lifted our burdens onto his own shoulders. We went off like straying sheep, while he went as a lamb to the slaughter, silent and uncomplaining.

53:11b-12. In at least five different ways God bears a witness to the servant's sufferings as a blessing for many.

Strangely and terribly, suffering is often the price ordained if light and truth and compassion are to be let loose among us. Sorrow is the lot of anyone who dares to be an outspoken advocate of strangers, foreigners, the poor, and the marginal. Any citizen who has a good word for the country's enemies, even infant enemies, will quickly discover the meaning of suffering. Martyrs have their lives snuffed out for holding up unwelcome light. Prophets suffer ridicule (and worse) for uttering uncomfortable truths.

Strange power flows from the acts of God's weak servants, God's poor martyrs, God's vulnerable prophets. Their sorrows accomplish what coercive force cannot. Their sufferings are the birthpangs of blessing for the rest of us.

THE WAY OF THE CROSS

In spite of New Age claims to the contrary, there is no fast path to bliss. At least the New Testament does not offer one. Rather, the path is narrow, hard, and sometimes excruciatingly slow. But the path does lead to bliss and is indeed full of blessing all the way.

Each Friday in Jerusalem at three in the afternoon, pilgrims gather for prayer in the courtyard of the Omariyyeh School at the northern edge of the temple mount. From there they set out along the Sorrowful Way (Via Dolorosa) or Way of the Cross, winding through the narrow streets of the Old City amid the cries of shopkeepers and the smells of spice and sewage until they reach the Church of the Holy Sepulchre covering Golgotha and Jesus' tomb.

That weekly rehearsal of Jesus' own Good Friday march bearing the cross has the same basic shape as the more joyous Palm Sunday procession with its emblems of triumph, and both conform to the contours of the whole historical way of Jesus as he moved from Galilee along the path to the city of his destiny. Good Friday, Palm Sunday, and his whole life were a journey through time toward his goal.

Holy Week walks are a tradition also outside Jerusalem. A famous via dolorosa was founded in Vilnius, Lithuania, in the seventeenth century. Thirty-six chapels were built along a five-mile stretch of road. One day in 1962 the political authorities dynamited all thirty-six chapels. When worshipers howled in protest, the authorities tried to justify the action by saying they merely wished to widen the highway and bring it up to modern standards.

If we do not walk the way of the cross with Jesus, what way are we traveling, and what map do we follow to find our way through the territory of our daily life?

Easter Vigil
Saturday of Light

Lutheran	Roman Catholic	Episcopal	Common Lectionary
Gen. 1:1—2:3	Gen. 1:1—2:2	Gen. 1:1—2:2	Gen. 1:1—2:2
Gen. 22:1-18	Gen. 22:1-18	Gen. 22:1-18	Gen. 22:1-18
Exod. 14:10—15:1	Exod. 14:10—15:1	Exod. 14:10—15:1	Exod. 14:10—15:1
Isa. 55:1-11	Isa. 55:1-11	Isa. 55:1-11	Isa. 55:1-11
Col. 3:1-4	Rom. 6:3-11	Rom. 6:3-11	Rom. 6:3-11
Matt. 28:1-10	Matt. 28:1-10	Matt. 28:1-10	Matt. 28:1-10

In the Easter Vigil the church takes its stand with the women at Jesus' tomb and waits, and while it waits it meditates on the path that brought him to that tomb and through it to newness of life. In Egeria's time and for many centuries, the Easter Vigil was the premier occasion, if not the only time, for baptisms with their offer of new life through burial in water.

According to Egeria, catechumens in fourth-century Jerusalem were enrolled at the beginning of Lent, vouched for by their godparents in the presence of the bishop. In the seven weeks preceding Great Week, the catechumens were instructed each morning from six until nine. Instruction began with lectures on the Scriptures. Later lectures focused on the Creed. During Great Week candidates participated in all the special services, culminating in their baptisms at the Easter Vigil. Egeria describes the baptisms as the chief element in the Vigil.

Cyril's *Catechetical Lectures* confirm the basic outline of the picture we have in Egeria's diary. Once the catechumens were enrolled, they were known as *photizomenoi,* "people in the process of being enlightened." After Easter they were further instructed in "mystagogical lectures," unfolding for them the full meaning of baptism.

The Easter Vigil today does not ordinarily call for a sermon. It is a service compounded of four chief elements: Kindling of Light, Readings of Scripture, Baptism of Candidates, and the Holy Communion.

KINDLING OF LIGHT

In Egeria's time, lamps and candles were lighted at vespers each day from fire brought out from within the tomb of Christ, where a lamp burns continuously day and night. In subsequent centuries the kindling of light on Easter Eve developed into the annual miracle of the Holy Fire, an event that occurs to this day. On Holy Saturday (which came to be known as the Saturday of Light or Saturday of Glory) all lamps and candles in the church are extinguished. While the faithful wait, each Holy Saturday around noon fire suddenly breaks out in the tomb of Jesus. The patriarch then passes fire from the tomb to those assembled, who share it excitedly, so that the whole gloomy space quickly blazes with light. Bernard offered an explanation in his *Itinerary* of 870, the first written account of the Holy Fire: "An angel comes in and kindles light in the lamps above the sepulchre."

Another account of the Holy Fire has been preserved in the diary of a Russian pilgrim, Abbot Daniel, from 1106. He tells how he left three lamps in the tomb on Good Friday and recovered them ablaze with light after the ceremony of the Holy Fire. With his lighted lamps he departed for home, traveling by boat along the coast to Constantinople and thence northward into Russia.

Today worshipers at Easter Vigils gather outside their sanctuaries in darkness and silence. New fire is struck and the paschal candle is lighted. Worshipers light their candles from the paschal candle and follow it into the dark sanctuary, like Israel marching in the wilderness behind the pillar of fire. Entering, they hear the threefold chant "The Light of Christ" (or "Christ Is Our Light"), and all respond, "Thanks be to God!"

The paschal candle is set before the altar, and the Exultet, a traditional hymn of praise to Christ as Light, or some other hymn of praise to God for the victory in Jesus Christ, is sung. All candelabra in the sanctuary are lit from the paschal candle. Worshipers extinguish their individual candles and settle down for the readings.

READINGS OF SCRIPTURE

The number of readings will vary. In ancient times twelve passages were read: Gen. 1:1—3:24; Gen. 22:1-18; Exod. 12:1-24; Jon. 1:1—4:11; Exod. 14:24—15:21; Isa. 60:1-13; Job 38:1-28; 2 Kings 2:1-22; Jer. 31:31-34; Josh. 1:1-9; Ezek. 37:1-14; Dan. 3:1-90 (The Song

of the Three Children). In addition, 1 Cor. 15:1-11 and Matt. 28:1-20 served as epistle and Gospel at the Eucharist.

The lectionaries we are following provide for six lessons, four to be read during the Service of Readings and the last two as epistle and Gospel in the Service of Communion.

Both ancient and contemporary lessons rehearse the entirety of God's history with the cosmos, stretching from creation's first dawning to its last day, from "In the beginning" (Genesis 1) to "the close of the age" (Matt. 28:20).

The readings bear witness to the struggle (even agony) out of which new life is born: light piercing darkness but continually threatened by the dark (Genesis 1), freedom wrested from slavery (Exodus 14–15), life surging up out of the sea (Genesis 1; Exodus 14–15), life rescued from under the knife (Genesis 22), life rising up from the soil (Isaiah 55) or bursting from the tomb (Matthew 28) or leaping up from the waters of baptism (Romans 6).

FIRST LESSON: GENESIS 1:1—2:3
PILGRIMAGE TOWARD THE SABBATH OF GOD

The psalmist declares that by merely speaking the word and exhaling the divine breath, God caused the world to spring instantly into being (Ps. 33:6). Genesis describes God's own journey through the first week, the primeval week, as a time of toiling capped by a day of resting.

In the beginning God stands before a dark and water chaos, formless and empty, hostile and forbidding, raging to no good purpose. The divine storm broods over that dark mass holding it in check. Then God's voice cracks through the silence: "Light, arise and shine!" "Waters, give way and make room." God's word creates light and order, triumphing over inky darkness and setting bounds to the unruly waters.

Thus light and air and solid land arise. Green plants appear on the dry land. By God's creative speaking, all these are shaped into a home for God's many creatures: the great lights ruling day and night, fish swarming in the seas and birds in the air, animals prowling the dry land, and human beings standing upright on the earth.

In a large and shining space, opened up in the midst of the darkness and the waters, God speaks words of promise and loves into existence a peaceable kingdom. Only then does God rest.

That first week is not only first but primordial. It lies not only before all other weeks but under them. It tells not only what God did but what God is doing even now.

Genesis is a call to worship, to hope, and to pilgrimage on the path from chaos to creation, from darkness to light, from struggle to the sabbath of God.

SECOND LESSON: GENESIS 22:1-18
ABRAHAM'S HARD JOURNEY

It was a hard journey for Abraham. And for Sarah? Was she still laughing? Not this time.

Ancient rabbis and some modern scholars discern in the narratives of Abraham ten episodes of testing punctuated by divine blessing after divine blessing. The climactic test is the summons to sacrifice Isaac. Here Abraham is not commanded to give up some trinket he owns or some precious possession outside himself. God does not speak here of a tithe of the harvest or some percentage of the flocks. This is Abraham's son, bone of his bone and flesh of his flesh. Isaac is his very life, and as an only son, Isaac is Abraham's only hope for a future.

Abraham had met all previous tests, but this last one is most terrible. It cuts to the bone. Will Abraham find the strength to render up his life to God? Is his life truly at God's disposal? Does he trust that in every circumstance God wills life?

This narrative of Abraham seems too harsh, too primitive, too mean for contemplation at baptism conducted to the strains of organ music in a church bathed in flickering candlelight. What does the sacrifice of Isaac have to do with baptism—our own or our children's?

In this awful narrative, the powers of chaos seem ready to burst their bonds and undo the Creator's good gift of life. Is God our creator or killer? What is this sacrifice that Abraham must make? And what is this drowning to which God calls us? Will this water kill us? Will it be the end of the real me, or my true beginning? What of my child on whom I pin so many hopes? Do I want what God wants for my child? Do I plan and know better than God? When we bring our children to baptism, they become in some profound sense separate from us. They may still live with us and for a long time depend on us, but at baptism they really do move into a new family. They move under the protection and direction of God "from whom every family in heaven

57

and on earth is named" (Eph. 3:15). They attain membership in the larger family of the pilgrim people of God.

Abraham's life was a pilgrim's journey toward Mount Moriah. Moriah came to be identified as the mountain where King Solomon built the temple (2 Chron. 3:1) in Jerusalem. Christians equated Moriah with Golgotha, and today there is a chapel of Saint Abraham in the Church of the Holy Sepulchre.

Moriah, temple mount, and Golgotha share spiritual space in Jerusalem, the goal of Jesus' pilgrimage. Jesus yielded up his life, not only at the cross on his final Friday but each step of the way. He was blessed with new life, not only at Easter but in each lap of his journey.

Moriah (vv. 2, 8, 14) means "God will see to it; God will provide." Each day God bids the pilgrim, "Give me your life," and God promises, "You will not die but live."

THIRD LESSON: EXODUS 14:10—15:1
PILGRIMAGE TOWARD FREEDOM

Exodus means escaping from tyrants and quitting slavery by abandoning security and stepping out in freedom and risk. Exodus means walking through water and through desert places, daring, adventuring, enduring. Finally, Exodus means arriving, entering, claiming the promise, singing to the Lord a new song.

The lesson opens on a note of despair and closes with a triumphant song of gladness. Israel was trapped between Pharaoh and the deep Red Sea. The households of Israel with all their flocks and herds had turned their backs on Egypt. Death had passed over them, and their slavery lay behind them. The Lord had gone before them, in a cloud by day and a pillar of fire by night (Exod. 13:21-22). They had begun their journey surrounded by miracles, but in a few short days they felt their freedom slipping away.

Pharaoh and his advisors had shaken off the plagues and the deaths of all their firstborn. They now regretted the loss of their former slaves and rose up, determined to establish the old order once more. Blinded by pride, Pharaoh found new courage (14:5-9).

Israel also experienced a change of heart. Seeing Pharaoh's chariots and his advancing army poised like a hammer to smack them against the anvil of the sea, they forgot the terrors of slavery. The grace of death's passage over them was a fading dream. They cried out in fear and complaint (14:10-12).

Moses had described the way before them as the path of freedom and new life. They had painted their doorposts, eaten the lamb, and ventured forth from Egypt, following Moses. Now suddenly their horizon was crowded with the chariots and horses of Pharaoh. They longed for the huts and hovels of their old lives as Pharaoh's slaves.

Moses addressed them confidently. "The Lord will fight for you!" (Exod. 14:14). Pharaoh and God entered into combat for the souls and bodies of the people.

The glorious cloud burning the way before Israel moved to the rear, obscuring Pharaoh's way. Moses lifted his staff, and a strong wind pushed back the waters of the sea. The children of Israel crossed over as if on dry ground, but the wheels of Egyptian chariots bogged down in the mud. Returning waters of the dark sea caught Pharaoh's soldiers, throwing them into panic.

The Israelites praised the Lord and then continued their journey. The angel of the Lord went before and behind, as vanguard and rearguard, in cloud every day and fire every night.

"Be still," Moses had said at the edge of the water. Quietly following God always leads to freedom and life, while life under Pharaoh is never anything but slavery and death.

FOURTH LESSON: ISAIAH 55:1-11
FOOD FOR THE JOURNEY

This triumphant hymn of gladness stands in the Easter Vigil as fitting climax to the dramas of creation, of Abraham and Isaac, and of the exodus from Egypt. It caps those readings and offers new creation, redemption, and freedom in baptism: "Ho, everyone who thirsts, come to the waters!"

In its own literary context, the hymn sums up the central theme of Isaiah 40–55: Listen! Because of God's sheer grace and unquenchable mercy, you stand on the threshold of a new age!

Beginning (1-2) and end (12-13) sound like the Christmas carol with the great verse "He comes to make his blessings flow far as the curse is found" ("Joy to the World"). No more will they eat bread by the sweat of their brow or fight a losing battle against thorns and thistles (Gen. 3:17-19).

The final verses of the hymn (12-13) are omitted from the lesson, probably because the powerful images might too easily fix our minds on material benefits: mountains bursting into song and trees of the field clapping their hands and the earth producing only greenery pleasing to the eye or good for food.

The opening verses offer a banquet (Isa. 25:6) of bread and beverages in free abundance. This free "food" is a fresh covenant relation with God, the gift of new life in the presence of God. It is free for the asking, free for the seeking (2-5). Seeking the Lord means forsaking paths of wickedness and setting our feet on godly paths. But what are they?

The Godness of God, higher than humanity, is not defined in terms of great power, endless knowledge, or infinite being. The Godness of God is described this way: "God will abundantly pardon."

God's path and God's thinking are "higher" than ours. How so? God does not store up grudges the way we do. God does not turn away, does not cease caring, never forgets a promise, never speaks an idle word.

The word that goes forth from the mouth of God travels a life-giving path. Like rain and snow from the heavens, it falls to earth upon Israel and the nations, rich and poor, just and unjust (Matt. 5:43-48). The waters of heaven make the earth green with wheat and then golden with ripe grain, giving seed to the sower and bread for the eater. Jesus compared himself to that seed (John 12, Tuesday) and to that bread from the hand of the divine Giver (Maundy Thursday).

The bread and water, wine and milk (Isa. 55:1-2) are God's word, God's wisdom, God's own being. That strong food sustains God's people in their pilgrimage day by day (Lord's Prayer, Matt. 6:11).

CELEBRATION OF BAPTISM

In traditional Easter Vigils the readings are followed by the singing of "The Song of the Three Children" ("*Benedicite, ombia opera*"; Additions to Daniel 3; LBW Canticle 18), the hymn sung by the three young men preserved from harm in the fiery furnace. As the canticle is sung, the paschal candle is carried to the baptismal font.

Egeria reports that the church at Jerusalem observes the Paschal Vigil exactly as she was accustomed to keeping the Vigil in her home on the Atlantic coast, with one exception. Immediately after the "infants" (new Christians) are baptized and clothed, they go in procession with the bishop to the Anastasis (the rotunda covering the tomb of Jesus).

Nowhere else in the world could a bishop approach the actual tomb of Jesus to pray on behalf of the newly baptized. After prayer in that holy spot, bishop and baptized together return to the Martyrium (basilica), rejoining the congregation and completing the vigil with the first Eucharist of Easter.

EASTER COMMUNION

The Eucharistic portion of the Vigil may begin with the singing of the Gloria. The liturgy of the Communion is brief and simple. Readings from the epistle and the Gospel climax the series of Scriptures that began with the narrative of creation in Genesis.

EPISTLE: ROMANS 6:3-11
(COLOSSIANS 3:1-4, LUTHERAN)

All worshipers—newly baptized and those baptized decades earlier—listen to Paul describe the spiritual life as a "walking." This image appears most frequently in Romans and Colossians, sources for our lessons (Rom. 6:4; 8:4; 13:13; 14:15; Col. 1:10; 2:6; 3:7; 4:5). The image is as old as 2 Kings 20:3 (the death speech of King Hezekiah) and plays a significant role in Proverbs (8:20 connects "walking" and "the way"). Elsewhere Paul picks up the pace and speaks of Christian life as "running" (Rom. 9:16; 1 Cor. 9:24, 26; Phil. 2:16; Gal. 2:2; 5:7; cf. Heb. 12:1, Wednesday).

In Romans 6 Paul does not define "walking in newness of life" (6:4). Elsewhere he does attend to the business of definition, fitting the image to the specific issues with which he and his congregations are struggling at the moment. He will get to that sort of thing in Romans 12–15.

But here in chap. 6 Paul is responding to a fundamental question he can hear rising up in the heart of his readers: "Doesn't all your talk about God's grace actually undermine efforts to walk in newness of life?"

Paul feels the force of the question (cf. Rom. 3:8). In response he lays bare the foundations of his own thinking. As he proceeds, he will argue on the basis of legal contracts and death (chap. 7) and he will fix attention on the experience of the Spirit (chap. 8). But he starts with baptism.

"Grace" is not simply some free-floating attitude of God, moving through the atmosphere above believers' heads. It is not even enough to say that baptism is an event that wrenched us alive out of Adam's shoes and set us down alive in the shoes of Christ Jesus. It is more convulsive an event than that.

Paul contemplates connections between the deep waters of baptism and the hard soil of Jesus' grave. The baptized are joined to Christ Jesus in his dying, in his falling down, in his being covered over and buried.

With Christ the baptized die out on the Adamic reality of the old age ruled by sin and death. They no longer belong to it. No more are they governed by its dynamics or moved by its impulses. They have been removed from its field of force.

The baptized now have power to walk according to the Spirit and not according to the flesh (Rom. 8:4). It's as though they had been transported to the moon, where earth's gravity does not prevail, or as though they had migrated to an entirely new country with new customs and new laws.

Paul does not here use the language of "body of Christ." He will come to that in chapter 12. But he is at pains here to speak the language of organic connection and integral participation.

We participate in Christ's death, and so we will participate in his resurrection. The future tense (in 6:5 and 6:8) seems to be emphatic. We have not yet arrived at the fullness of the new resurrection life. But we can and we will even now before the time begin to "walk in newness of life" (6:4). We are on the way, even though all our movements are faltering baby steps.

Christ has conquered death, and it has forever lost its power over him and over all who belong to him. Connected with Christ, the baptized believer is moving along the road from death to life.

GOSPEL: MATTHEW 28:1-10, 16-20

It would be easy enough to compose a roll call of villains, a dark counterpart of the honor roll of saints in Hebrews 11. It might begin with Cain or with Pharaoh of Exodus, continue with Israelite monarchs like Ahab and Jezebel and Manasseh, include foreign rulers like Nebuchadnezzar and Antiochus IV, and climax with Herod and Pilate. Not just evil individuals but the power of evil itself is on the march, unwearied and relentless, forming a kind of antipilgrimage.

The crucifixion of Jesus was the world's deadly no to the Creator of life and light. God's world wanted to organize itself on lines of its own choosing. God's prodigal self-giving, mirrored in the sun's rising each day on good and evil, in the rain's falling on the just and the unjust alike, and in Jesus' eating with tax collector and sinner, was judged to be too risky and too odd. The divine love was weighed and found wanting. Jesus was examined and rejected, crucified and buried.

But God did not let Jesus drop. God did not permit evil or "common sense" to have the last word. In a burst of light like the world's first morning, God summoned Jesus up out of death, out of the arms of chaos, out of the earth, as the firstborn among many sisters and brothers.

Matthew is emphatic. A great stone, as heavy as death, mocking God's word of life and halting Jesus' further progress, was set and sealed and securely guarded (27:65-66). On Easter it was thrust aside by earthquake and angel, indeed by "great earthquake" and "angel of the Lord." That means that God had done it and no human being.

The empty tomb is a great gaping hole in human assumptions and human calculations. It is a yawning crater left by the explosive act of God. It is a giant footprint in solid rock testifying that God has passed this way.

Easter is an act of power; but even more, it expresses God's unconquered mercy. By raising up Jesus, God says yes to Jesus and no to the crucifying powers. Yes to Jesus' healing touch, to his outrageous habit of forgiving sinners and welcoming infants and receiving outcasts. Yes to Jesus' preference for mercy over fussy ritual and the exacting details of a puritanic code. No to those who place class and nation and religious tradition above God. No to those who pursue personal piety and ignore the basic needs of the neighbor.

In fact, the resurrection of Jesus means that no ray of light, no loving deed, no act of mercy, no word of forgiveness is ever lost or defeated. God sees and affirms them. They are woven into the fabric of the new creation, and they will shine forever (Matt. 13:43).

Women came out expecting to see a tomb sealed with a stone but found the angel of the Lord atop the stone beside an open grave. The same angel was there at Jesus' beginning (1:20, 24; 2:13, 19). God broods over Jesus' entrance into our ordinary life and at his exit from it. God stands at those mysterious gateways of Jesus' life, giving and receiving his being.

Jesus' resurrection promises that all our beginnings and endings lie in the hands of God. What and who we are is not determined by chemistry and biology alone but by the God who gave Jesus and who raised Jesus. God is the fountain and the goal of our life.

Women came looking for a corpse. They came out to pay their final respects to their dear, dead friend. The angel gave them a word of new life, and that word is the heart of the Gospel reading: "He has been raised just as he said." The end of all his living and teaching and healing is not death but new life.

In John's account of Easter (chap. 20), Jesus appears to Thomas, inviting him to touch the wounds. In Matthew's narrative, only the women touch Jesus. Falling on their knees before him and bending low, they seize his feet. It is an act of reverence, mirroring the respect paid to Jesus at the beginning of the Gospel by the Magi (2:11). It is reverence denied him in the beginning by Herod and in the end by Pilate, who fixed his feet with nails to a cross.

In grasping his feet, the women articulate their reverence in a fashion perfectly matching the theme of this brief commentary on the lessons of Holy Week. They express unconditional respect for Jesus and for the way he has walked: "How beautiful are his feet."

The stone has been thrust aside, and the crucified, raised up to new life, goes on his way. He moves now as one who has been given all authority, at the head of a vast body of pilgrims. They are called to be disciples and to make disciples, trusting that their origin and their destiny are in life-giving hands.

God's creative word of life and light and love has at Easter once again pierced the gloom and ordered the chaos. Jesus, as God's healing presence, walks with all pilgrims all the way to the end of days.